TRANSGENDER IDENTITY

TRANSGENDER
IDENTITY

A View Through a Wide Angle Lens

Joseph W. Needham, Ph.D.

ELM HILL

A Division of
HarperCollins Christian Publishing

www.elmhillbooks.com

Transgender Identity

A View through a Wide Angle Lens

Published in Nashville, Tennessee, by Elm Hill, an imprint of Thomas Nelson. Elm Hill and Thomas Nelson are registered trademarks of HarperCollins Christian Publishing, Inc.

Elm Hill titles may be purchased in bulk for educational, business, fund-raising, or sales promotional use. For information, please e-mail SpecialMarkets@ ThomasNelson.com.

Library of Congress Cataloging-in-Publication Data

ISBN 978-1-400326617 (Paperback)
ISBN 978-1-400326624 (Hardbound)
ISBN 978-1-400326631 (eBook)

DEDICATION

My parents rejoice in the humanly unimaginable and indescribable holiness of the Savior's presence. Yet the Godly influence they planted and nourished while on earth continues to reap rewards and remains as an endearing testament to the Father's everlasting faithfulness, mercy, and grace.

This book is dedicated to their memory.

ACKNOWLEDGMENTS

This project has been on my mind for some time. Were it not for the encouragement from family, friends, colleagues, fellow pastors and others, it would never have come to fruition. My first and foremost gratitude goes to Sybil, my wife, who in many respects co-wrote this book. Moreover, her support and companionship throughout the experience was clearly providential. Secondly is our adult child, River, of whom we are immensely proud and pleased to claim as our own. Tom Needham, Rosanne Foster, Dr. David Needham, and Mary Swartz read part or all of the manuscript and provided helpful insights. Dr. Carol Hester's observant eye brought a number of critical issues to my attention. Dr. John Ernst's notable suggestions resulted in a more discerning monograph. I'm grateful to my colleagues and friends Gail Heying, Dr. Darko Zidlar, and Dr. Wade Shilts who were kind enough to examine and comment on the book. Thank you also to the team at Elm Hill Publishers whose prodding and suggestions were immensely helpful. Any errors within these pages are solely mine.

Ridgeway, Iowa, April 10, 2020

NOTE ON THE TITLE

Two terms were considered seriously in naming the book. The first was Transgenderism, but in the interests of compassion and understanding the second descriptor, Transgender Identity was utilized. Its incorporation was not an arbitrary decision, nor was it easily made. Instead it resulted from considerable research, contemplation, meditation, prayer, and deliberation. Many terms carry baggage, transgenderism is no exception. One needs only to peruse websites such as Reddit, Quora, www.glaad.org/reference/transgender, and many others to secure a plethora of opinions. Some find no problem with it, while others are deeply offended. Indeed, popular author, Sheila Jeffreys, penned *Gender Hurts: A Feminist Analysis of the Politics of Transgenderism*, Perhaps the strongest evidence for using transgenderism is based on the position held by the World Professional Association for Transgender Health. According to its website, the organization's purpose is "to promote evidence-based care, education, research, advocacy, public policy, and respect in transgender health." Moreover, its primary publication, *The International Journal of Transgenderism,* "is a quarterly peer-reviewed academic journal covering research on gender dysphoria, the medical and psychological treatment of transgender individuals, social and legal acceptance of sex reassignment, and professional and public education on transgenderism." Nevertheless, significant opposition to the term exists so in lieu of it Transgender Identity is placed. Although some will undoubtedly disagree, the term transgender identity is incorporated into the book title and used throughout.

CONTENTS

Contents

CHAPTER 1

THE MATTER AT HAND

Grace to you and peace from God our Father and the Lord Jesus
Christ.

Blessed be the God and Father of our Lord Jesus Christ, the
Father of mercies and God of all comfort; who comforts us in all
our affliction so that we may be able to comfort those who are in
any affliction with the comfort which we ourselves are comforted
by God.

2 CORINTHIANS 1:2–4[1]

During the past few years, a greater openness has arisen in evangelical circles regarding the avalanche of intensely personal
problematic issues that the Lord allows many Christians to experience.
Clearly, everyone encounters unanticipated challenges on the road of

---

[1] Charles Caldwell Ryrie, *The Ryrie Study Bible New American Standard Version*
(Chicago: Moody Press, 1995). All Scripture passages in this monograph are quoted
from the *New American Standard Bible*, 1995 revision.

life. Marital conflict, financial pressures, occupational difficulties, sibling rivalries, and general relational discord are part of living in a fallen world. As sin-tainted beings, humans reap the consequences of disobedience, rebellion, and defiance toward the Father. Scripture is explicit in explaining that "all have sinned and fall short of the glory of God." In fact, the Lord Jesus Himself states that "there is only One who is good." Sin affects everyone and sin's effects are manifested in people's lives around the globe. In some families, relationships, and individuals, the obvious consequences of a fallen world may be more apparent than in others. For instance, many experience greater pain, grief, heartache, and loneliness than others. However, that does not in any way acknowledge, imply, or infer that they have sinned more than those who appear to agonize less.

Some will argue that perhaps those who suffer have "hidden sins" of which they think no one is aware. Yet one needs only to study the book of Job to observe the fallacy of such non-biblical albeit popular heresy. They may mention the scriptural principle of sowing and reaping; people reap what they sow, more than they sow, and later than they sow.[2] However, what those individuals do not grasp is that the Father may permit a heart-wrenching situation in some believers' lives so they can sow a Godly attitude and response for others to observe and emulate. Nevertheless, many believers cling to the concept that people cause their own challenges and trials by their conduct, conversation, or character. Granted, sometimes people experience self-inflicted difficulties, but often that is not the case. The apostle Peter in his first epistle 5:8 warned that Satan prowls about as a roaring lion seeking someone to devour. He can and

---

[2]   Charles F. Stanley, ed. *Life Principles Bible New American Standard Version* (Nashville: Thomas Nelson, 2005), xxi-xxii.

does wreak havoc in lives. All too often the wicked one uses well-meaning yet ill-advised Christians to prompt despair among believers by stating or implying that those who are in the midst of excruciating trials are merely receiving what they are due; not unlike the statements of Job's "friends." Some saints may feel encapsulated by what seems like a never-ending and ever-intensifying experience of deep grief, sadness, emotional pain, and hurt prompted by difficult or perhaps overwhelming circumstances. Many like Job, through no fault of their own, sense hopelessness and relate closely to his words spoken in desperation, "He has cast me into the mire, and I have become like dust and ashes. I cry out to You for help but You do not answer me; I stand up and You turn Your attention against me. You have become cruel to me; with the might of Your hand You persecute me."[3] Hopefully, reading this monograph will prove cathartic for those who can empathize with Job's emotional outburst. Perhaps some hurting soul will absorb a few morsels on which to meditate and begin the long, painful, and difficult but essential path toward healing.

When it became known that several evangelical pastors and others in our denominational association faced the unusual but not uncommon issues such as transgender identity, transsexual identity, gender dysphoria, homosexuality, non-binary sexual expression, and gender non-conforming people within their families, close relationships, and congregations, some wanted to help.[4] However, there appeared to be little, if any, pertinent material written from a biblical perspective. There was, however,

---

[3]   Job 30:19–21.

[4]   There are a host of words regarding non-binary sexual expression utilized throughout this book. The title includes only transgender identity, but the subject matter incorporates many more aspects of sexual non-conformity. Please see the glossary

plenty of information compiled from a purely secular standpoint. It was, to say the very least, antagonistic toward evangelicals, Holy Writ, and a Godly worldview. Hence, the Scriptures and other biblically based sources were searched to locate answers regarding how best to encourage those in need, to help them cope and progress through their circumstances. This book also incorporates secular sources with a left-wing sociocultural bias, and some on the right as well as ostensibly non-biased evidence. Some material was decidedly antagonistic toward evangelicalism while other sources viewed it sympathetically.[5]

Hence, this work is based upon what was gleaned from the Lord, other believers, as well as secular and Christian materials. It examines various components of transgender identity, transsexual identity, and non-binary sexual expression particularly as they affect the families, friends, and acquaintances of those who experience some component of gender dysphoria. They receive some treatment as well.

The consequences of relational or familial non-binary sexual expression for many families can become highly problematic. It affects some friends, family, and others associated closely with congregational leadership and many more who hold positions of authority within their respective churches. A scenario like this is not supposed to occur in families and others whose lives are centered on the Lord Jesus and His work. Yet while continuing on the path of reassurance, encouragement,

---

located at the end of the book for definitions of an abridged list of some relatively frequently used terminology.

[5]   Clearly, one could not integrate all available information without writing an extensive tome. Thus, much of the material examined but may not have been cited can be found in various footnotes or in the annotated bibliography.

and comfort, it becomes more and more apparent that pastors', deacons', elders', and various families in denominational leadership are exempt from nothing that the Father allows in His permissive will.[6] Indeed, the Lord sanctions these and similar challenges to orchestrate believers' complete dependence upon Him for their very being; a condition often referred to as brokenness. Unfortunately, the vast majority of evangelicals do not reach that state. However, those who never experience it cannot truly grasp the concept of total reliance upon God. But for those who do, it reveals an awesome yet humbling perspective of the Father, the Son, the Holy Spirit, themselves, and their life situation. It is attainable by no other method. Furthermore, the Lord often uses broken people in ways that are available to no one else.

These findings and understandings are shared because numerous believers closely associated with ministry find themselves in deeply troubling circumstances. Moreover, the number of families with a high view of God's Word confronted with non-binary sexual expression and related issues among their family, friends, or other close associates increases daily. Indeed, one frequently becomes apprised of yet another evangelical household faced with an analogous situation. Although the Father may

---

[6] God's Will may be divided into three categories; His perfect will, circumstantial will, and permissive will. His perfect will occurs when one trusts Christ as personal savior at an early age and lives in complete submission to Him. The Father's circumstantial will refers to those who reject the Lord for many years but in time put their faith in Him. They then live in obedience after wasting much of their life. The Creator's permissive will occurs when He allows trials to enter believers' lives or for Christians to make poor decisions but He uses the consequences for the saints' edification and spiritual growth. Thus one may discern the path that incorporates both God's sovereignty and human free will

seem far away as Job erroneously thought, that is a lie of Satan. The evil one wants those experiencing extreme trials to sense intense loneliness and isolation which can exacerbate the notion that no one understands their experience. He directs believers to the secular material that denies a biblical worldview and scriptural authority. That, in turn, tends to draw them continually deeper into Lucifer's abyss. He wants to destroy families and unfortunately has been quite successful. An important purpose of this work is to express the message that believers are never alone in their struggle; rather, there are many who face the aforementioned and comparable relational issues. Hebrews 13:5b reminds us "for He Himself has said 'I will never desert you, nor will I ever forsake you.'" Those in distress need to discuss their hurt, pain, and grief with the Father and other compassionate trustworthy believers to secure a resolution. The wicked one attacks pastors and their families as well as lay evangelicals in countless ways. Due to the evil one and his minions utilizing effectively their cunning strategies, many pastors, missionaries, and others in the Lord's work have been spiritually shipwrecked, forced from the ministry, lost their families, or experienced other terrible consequences. The Lord has been exceptionally gracious in that many have not encountered such abysmal results. However, He has allowed them to experience untold emotional pain, grief, and sorrow. Hence, this book is designed primarily for evangelical pastors and their families who have suffered, or are experiencing, deep relational or familial discord. It is also intended for those who may not be pastors but hold congregational leadership roles. Those who do not have a church position and others who hold a nebulous view of Scripture may find amelioration as well. Finally, someone who might not have a relationship with the Lord but has questions regarding transgender identity, transsexual identity, gender dysphoria, and related topics might find some answers. Perhaps an individual who wonders how knowing the Savior relates to these issues, will find this monograph helpful as well. Please be assured that in whatever category one may find herself or himself, they are not alone. Satan enjoys separating those in pain from other believers so he can drag them down and cause as much agony and doubt as possible. God, however, yearns for all to understand that He does not intend for saints to deal with these situations on their own. To find contentment along with a sense of purpose for their pain, grief, and sorrow, Christians must allow Him to take control and let His name be glorified. Just as Peter noted in his first epistle 5:6–7 as he wrote to persecuted and hurting believers, "Therefore humble yourselves under the mighty hand of God, that He may exalt you at the proper time, casting all your anxiety on Him, because He cares for you."

Although evangelicals in church leadership faced with close relational or familial gender dysphoria, transgender identity, transsexual identity, and similar acts of rebellion prompted this book's authorship, the fact remains that readers may relate it to any type of problematic non-scriptural behavior. The essential principles can be applied to other issues such as fornication, adultery, homosexuality, drug/alcohol addiction, criminal activity, abusive relationships, or a host of other un-Christlike actions. While perusing these pages seek from the Lord effective strategies to bring relational relief. Believers have been on the sidelines far too long as demonic-inspired pop culture and social mores have worked their way into evangelicals' lives, homes, families, circles of friends, acquaintances, and churches. It is past time to take an uncompromised stand for what is right and for what God says in His Word. Indeed, the psalmist wrote in

119:9: "How can a young man keep his way pure? By keeping it according to Your word." Furthermore, verse 105 of that chapter reads, "Your Word is a lamp to my feet and a light to my path." This piece is written from a perspective that maintains a high view of Scripture. It is the immutable, verbal, plenary, Holy Spirit–breathed, inerrant, infallible, and eternal Word of God.[7] It is "living, active, and sharper than any two-edged sword, piercing as far as the division of soul and spirit, of joint and marrow and able to judge the thoughts and intentions of the heart." Moreover, "The grass withers, the flower fades, but the word of our God stands forever."[8]

Perhaps someone might be thinking that their physical body does not reflect the gender by which they view themselves emotionally, spiritually, intellectually, or sexually. This is not an easy position for anyone. This publication's purpose is not in any way to offend or antagonize people. Rather, it is to be supportive, encouraging, and heartening. Hence, it offers suggestions that may not be located elsewhere. For instance, some have been told that changing one's physical body to match their emotional, intellectual, spiritual, or sexual perceptions will be an incredibly freeing experience. Nevertheless, no change in one's physical makeup or appearance will bring freedom, peace, or contentment. The Lord Jesus Himself said, "If you continue in My word, then you are truly disciples of Mine;

---

7   Charles Caldwell Ryrie, *A Synopsis of Bible Doctrine* (Chicago: Moody Press, 1965), Revised, 1995 "Doctrine of the Scriptures," p. 2055–2056 in Ryrie, *The Ryrie Study Bible.* For a more thorough discussion see Millard J. Erickson, *Christian Theology* (Grand Rapids: Baker Book House, 1993), pp. 153–259.

8   Hebrews 4:12; Isaiah 40:8.

and you will know the truth and the truth will make you free."[9] Believers long for all to be made free by the Lord Jesus Himself. Although evangelicals have been falsely labeled as exclusive, hateful, or bigoted because they generally do not issue *carte blanche* to those who reject their birth sex, the vast majority do not detest anyone. Nor are believers exclusive in any sense of the term. Nothing could be further from the Truth. Jesus is more inclusive than anyone. The Lord is "not wishing for any to perish but for all to come to repentance."[10] Rather, their love prevents them from acquiescing to the status quo. Evangelicals simply want all, especially friends, family members, loved ones, colleagues, acquaintances, and others to find their identity, peace, and contentment through the Lord Jesus.

Clearly, no simple answers or responses will resolve the issues of gender dysphoria, transgender identity, transsexual identity, or non-binary sexual expression and evaporate all associated emotional pain and discord. A complicated situation intensified by passionate expressions from various sources is not easily elucidated. A transgender, transsexual, or individual with gender dysphoria experiences inextricable pain, heartache, and grief; hence, they, along with these issues, are approached with compassion and understanding. Nevertheless, addressing and accepting the transgender, transsexual, or individual with gender dysphoria does not in any way infer, imply, or suggest approval of that person's behavior, mindset, or beliefs. Materials prepared by worldly authors contend that not approving a transgender as such represents prejudice and intolerance,

---

[9]   John 8:32–33.

[10]   2 Peter 3:9b.

among other derogatory descriptors.[11] That attitude is to be expected from those who do not have a close, personal, intimate, and growing relationship with the Savior. Quite frankly, the opposite of what most seculars write is true. The Lord Jesus died on the cross for all. Believers simply yearn that everyone is made aware of the truth and freedom that comes only from personally trusting in the Lord's atoning death alone to pay their sin debt in full. By doing so, one may be made free by the Son. As John 8:36 reads, "So if the Son makes you free you will be free indeed."

This subject is broached with vulnerable hearts, inquisitive minds, and exposed lives and pray that this work will be a cathartic source for all who experience the challenges addressed. Considerable Scripture is incorporated into the text because it is comforting and encouraging to read what God says in His Word. Psalm 119:97–98 expresses, "How I love Your law! It is my meditation all the day. Your commandments make me wiser than my enemies, for they are ever mine." Remember it is essential to be completely honest before the Lord to allow His healing to occur. Indeed, He knows one's feelings and attitudes better than they know themselves. As Holy Writ notes in 1 Chronicles 28:9a, "As for you, my son Solomon, know the God of your father, and serve Him with a whole heart, and a willing mind; for the Lord searches all hearts and understands every intent of the thoughts." Also, note King David's words in Psalm 139:1–4: "O Lord You have searched me and known me. You know when I sit down and when I rise up; You understand my thought from afar. You scrutinize my path and my lying down, and are intimately acquainted with all my ways. Even before there is a word on my tongue,

---

[11] Gary Kelly, *Sexuality Today, 10th ed.* (McGraw-Hill: New York, 2008), p. 193–200.

behold O Lord, You know it all." Hence, any attempt at hiding something from God is a fruitless endeavor.

Just as it is best for a physical wound to recover from the inside, emotional injuries cannot be healed by a scab covering a deep scar. Moreover, the popular adage that time heals all wounds is contrary to scriptural teachings as well as complete nonsense. Time does not heal anything. It simply creates a greater interval between the incident that precipitated the pain, grief, and heartache and the present. A look at some biblical passages composed by David under the inspiration of the Holy Spirit reveals a heartfelt outpouring from the depths of his soul to the Lord. After he was smitten with guilt for his adultery with Bathsheba and his murder of Uriah, he wrote in Psalm 38:1–2, "O Lord, rebuke me not in Your wrath, and chasten me not in Your burning anger. For Your arrows have sunk deep into me and your hand has pressed down on me." Verses 4 and 5 reveal that David accepted full responsibility for his sin, by which he provoked the Lord. "For my iniquities have gone over my head; as a heavy burden they weigh too much for me. My wounds grow foul and fester because of my folly." Another example of David's crying out to God is recorded in 1 Samuel 29:3–4 and 6. While he was dwelling with the Philistines in exile from Saul, he was not permitted to fight with them when they prepared for a major offensive against the Hebrews. Upon the return to his dwelling place in Ziklag, he learned that the Amalekites had raided the town and kidnapped its residents, his family along with those of his men. Holy Writ records that "David and the people who were with him lifted their voices and wept until there was no strength in them to weep"[12] Indeed, to make matters worse, David was greatly

---

[12]   1 Samuel 30:4.

distressed because his followers spoke of stoning him, "for all the people were embittered, each one because of his sons and his daughters. But David strengthened himself in the Lord his God"[13] Many, like David, have cried out to the Lord. He responded, but perhaps not with the expected or hoped for answer. God, however, provides grace, which is always sufficient. He has never abandoned any believer. Furthermore, He continues to draw His children ever closer unto Himself. The Lord's chief longing is to have a close, personal, intimate, and growing relationship with all and to draw believers closer to the God of all comfort.

When the Israelites asked Samuel to appoint for them a king, he was displeased and went to the Lord. In 1 Samuel 8:7, Scripture explains God's response: "The Lord said to Samuel, Listen to the voice of the people in regard to all that they say to you, for they have not rejected you, but they have rejected me from being king over them." The Father agreed to let the Israelites have their king, to be like other nations around them. Nevertheless, it was not in their best interest as God knew, but He wanted them to learn that truth for themselves. Often the Lord does the same today; He knows that experience is a great teacher. Its difficult but memorable exams often occur before the material is presented. Therefore, learners rarely forget its lasting lessons. God's Word reveals that the Lord knows what is best for all even if it runs contrary to public opinion as espoused by much of the media and pop culture. God does not run popularity contests regarding His will; neither should believers. Rather it is best to remain with His Word and His direction. He always knows what is best.

Indeed, when the children of Israel were being taken into captivity by

---

[13] 1 Samuel 30:6.

the Babylonians, the prophet Jeremiah noted in 29:10–11: "For thus says the Lord, 'When seventy years have been completed for Babylon, I will visit you and fulfill My good word to you, to bring you back to this place. For I know the plans that I have for you,' declares the Lord, 'plans for welfare and not for calamity to give you a future and a hope.'" The Father has a marvelous plan for all. Evangelicals simply need to seek Him and His Word to discern it. The subsequent verses that Jeremiah penned read, "Then you will call upon Me and come and pray to Me, and I will listen to you. You will seek Me and find Me when you search for Me with all your heart." The prophet concluded, "'I will be found by you,' declares the Lord, 'and I will restore your fortunes and will gather you from all the nations and from all the places where I have driven you, and I will bring you back to the place from where I sent you into exile.'"[14]

When gender dysphoria or related issues enter an evangelical's circle of friends, family, or colleagues, Satan often sends wicked thoughts that challenge the believer's relational skills. He often prompts doubts and regrets into their minds especially regarding how they in good faith may have affected the transgender individual. Yet the fact of the matter is that those who were influenced with an evangelical mindset typically can choose to reject what was taught and practiced and become transgender. This is part of a person's free will. Individuals are free moral agents. Parents bring up their children in the nurture and admonition of the Lord. Friends, family, and others often provide Godly influence as well. Nevertheless, a person will take the principles they were taught along with their experiences and do with them as they please. Indeed, the Bible clearly reveals that the Father provided explicit instructions for

---

[14] Jeremiah 27:12–14.

Adam and Eve. In a broad sense, one could say He reared them, but look what they did. Both deliberately disobeyed Him and ate the fruit of the tree of the knowledge of good and evil. Hence, Satan infers or even indicates that God is a negligent parent. If He failed in that task, how can He be trusted in any other? Examine, for instance, the godly judges of Eli and Samuel. Although their sons were reared knowing right from wrong, how to make proper sacrifices, and the importance of living for the Lord, they all rebelled against Him. Eli's sons were killed in battle because of their sin while Samuel's were rejected as judges. Satan sends to parents, friends, family, and others all kinds of distressing messages and lies to dishearten and foster disappointment along with discouragement. He challenges the Lord by saying that if He is God, then why does He allow these things to happen? Furthermore, the evil one prompts many family members to ask questions such as why will He not seem to answer their pleas before the Throne of Grace, heal their friend or family member and set them back on track. Satan separates those parents, friends, and family members from others by telling them what failures they are as parents, guardians, friends, acquaintances, siblings, and even as human beings. Yet it is up to them to reject messages from the father of lies.

Everyone's story is undoubtedly unique, but the gist is probably similar. Many believers have close friends, family, acquaintances, colleagues, and others whom they love dearly but abuse drugs, alcohol, or perhaps turned to crime, homosexuality, bisexuality, fornication, adultery, transgender identity, transsexual identity, lesbianism, or any of a host of non-biblically ordained lifestyles. Perhaps some evangelicals may have drifted so far from the Lord that they themselves have chosen that dark path. The fact of the matter is that many Christians struggle regarding someone for whom they love or care deeply who chooses to live in rebellion. They may be uneasy about sharing their situation with others and feel a deep sense of loneliness because no one understands their situation. But recall that a believer is not alone, the Lord will never leave or forsake His children, those who have put their faith and trust solely in His atoning death for their personal eternal salvation. Furthermore, the situations which He allows in one's life can also unite believers. Do not provide Satan the satisfaction of dispersing you to the world that approves and promotes God-dishonoring behavior. Rather, stand together in the power of the Lord and in the strength of His might put on the full armor of God and withstand the wiles of the devil.

As implied by the title, this piece takes a multidisciplinary approach to the issues of transgender identity, transsexual identity, gender dysphoria, non-binary sexual attraction along with other un-Christlike behaviors. Psychology, philosophy, communication, history, biology, and sociology are all addressed to some degree. Each chapter treats a separate issue that the Lord brought to mind as an evangelical academician and pastor. Many other facets exist, all of which deserve analysis. They do, however, exceed the parameters addressed here. Hopefully, these few thoughts will provide assistance and direction for those struggling in one way or another with some component of gender dysphoria and its manifestations.

Following an introduction in the Matter at Hand, discussion focuses on the role that feelings have in transsexual identity, transgender identity, and gender dysphoria. As created beings, people have emotions that comprise a major component of one's humanity. However, they sometimes get out of hand, creating a situation that dishonors the Lord. Hence, an entire chapter, Emotional Turmoil in Relational Transgender Identity, deals with that very issue and explains how God empowers His own to maintain control of their feelings.

When one considers the cultural and social change of the past century, it is absolutely mind-boggling. The 1890s, for example, were for most of the twentieth century often described as the "Gay Nineties." Yet fast forward to the 1990s and one sees an entirely different scenario unthinkable 100 years previous. Perceptions surrounding the term "gay" changed dramatically. The concept of absolute truth is generally not taught nor expressed in post-modern culture and society, while cultural relativism, pragmatism, and pluralism are popular topics. A perceptive person is prompted to ponder what could have happened philosophically and theologically in the world and the United States to facilitate this monumental change. The chapter titled Philosophical, Theological, and Historical Foundations of Transgender Identity delves into this development.

Much attention is given to the notion that science says people are born homosexual or transgender or in some condition that the Bible says is sin. Hence, various questions emerge such as: What does science truly say about the matter? What do the studies actually reveal? From where or by whom are the projects funded? What about their reliability and validity? Who conducts the peer-reviewed projects? Who are the peers? How are these studies portrayed in the media? An examination of the studies themselves, rather than what others have reported, is addressed in the chapter Scientific Evidence Regarding Gender Dysphoria, Transgender Identity, and Transsexual Identity.

How does one who is faced with relational gender nonconformity in any of its various manifestations come to terms with it? Often families, friends, associates, and others close to the transgender perceive a deep sense of loss. The individual they knew and loved is apparently gone and someone has taken their place. Grief often follows. The world says that by accepting the situation, one can process it and not flounder in despair. However, is that response congruent with Scripture? A chapter titled Does Acceptance Truly Bring Relief? explores this intriguing query.

Is there any means by which transgenders, transsexuals or those experiencing gender dysphoria can find some common ground with those who find those issues highly problematic? If so, may the affected parties then seek the Lord's will and direction? Loud accusations and condemnation from either side do little more than elevate people's emotional level and prompt even greater division. Furthermore, it is incumbent upon believers to recall that the Lord allows challenging situations, events, circumstances, and the like to mature one's faith. Thus, one chapter, A Problem or an Opportunity for Growth?, addresses that very topic.

In cases where an individual is particularly close to someone, the question often arises regarding communication. Humans are social beings made for relationship. Yet at times maintaining a connection can become onerous. Should it continue and at what cost, or should it cease? Heartbreak results from learning or reading of the pain and sorrow of those who abandoned their family and friends or of those whose loved ones and others rejected them. Communication is clearly an issue that deserves and receives an entire chapter.

Believers should be cognizant of the fact that the Lord wants them to grow in their walk with Him. One of the more effective ways that this can happen is to be led by Him through some dark valleys, rough waters, and experience deep emotional pain that distresses one's very spirit and soul. Families and friends of a transgender, a transsexual, someone experiencing gender dysphoria or some other state that contradicts Scripture often find themselves deep in those chasms or on choppy, storm-tossed seas. Therefore, an astute individual will seek to learn what God is teaching them. If one has to endure such a difficult and painful experience, it is prudent to allow the Father to show one what He has to teach. Therefore, a chapter, Lessons from the Lord, is devoted to that discussion.

Sometimes after reading a book, one is challenged to consider exactly what to take from it. This is especially true when the piece discusses deeply personal and emotionally charged material. One may feel at somewhat of a loss regarding how to put everything together and move forward. Therefore, the final chapter consists of several significant ideas that one may glean from the book as well as suggestions for the future.

In essence, the first portion of the monograph describes the "what is" regarding non-binary sexual attraction while the second half is more practical with various suggestions, focused primarily on how to facilitate one's personal walk with God. Rather than point fingers and find fault, look inward, confess, repent, and forsake sin. Learn to thrive under trials and difficult circumstances. Allow the Father to use those situations in one's life as well as the life of the transgender and seek His face for wisdom and insight. Ask Him to reveal the lessons He is teaching. Allow the Father, the Word, as well as the Holy Spirit to use those truths to mold one into the image of the Lord Jesus; by doing so, this book will have accomplished its primary purpose.

CHAPTER 2

EMOTIONAL TURMOIL IN RELATIONAL TRANSGENDER IDENTITY

Let your forbearing spirit be known to all men. The Lord is near.
Be anxious for nothing, but in everything by prayer and supplication let your requests be made known to God. And the peace of
God, which surpasses all comprehension, shall guard your hearts
and your minds in Christ Jesus.

PHILIPPIANS 4:5–7

From the instant of their creation, humans were blessed with emotions
as a component of personhood. Before the fall, their feelings were all
positive, affirming, constructive, and honored the Lord. Indeed, following
His work God said that all elements of creation were good. Perfection pervaded the Garden of Eden. Adam and Eve were in complete and untainted

fellowship with God as well as each other. All three relished the relationship. Satan, however, determined to destroy the communion between humans and God, tempted Eve, who prompted Adam to make a deliberate, willful, and cognitive choice to disobey his Creator's command. Thus, sin entered into the picture and destroyed the perfect fellowship between God and His human creation. A major consequence of Adam's behavior was the cataclysmic alteration of the previously unblemished emotions with which he and Eve were entrusted. Negative sentiments immediately emerged. Anger, guilt, blame, anguish, and shame were merely a few that appeared before that day ended. Those and other adverse feelings are but samples with which many may become quite familiar during the earlier stages of learning to deal with relational or familial transgender identity.

Clearly, not everyone faced with that situation will experience all these emotions. Scripture communicates that humans (including our emotional makeup) are "fearfully and wonderfully made."[15] In that process, some will have a strong sensation of certain emotions, while others may not feel them at all but instead need to process different ones. There is not a one-size-fits-all modality when dealing with emotions. With that being said, research, observation, as well as communication with those in similarly difficult circumstances all indicate that these five are perhaps among the more common. It is essential to remember that the emotions here are treated in no particular order.

Anger is, for many, a natural reaction when faced with unplanned situations or crises that they cannot control. Since the fall, humans often aspire to be in charge. American culture and society promote freedom and autonomy so each person can generally engage in what they yearn

---

[15] Psalm 139:14a.

to do, be what they want to be, or think what they desire to think—all in the process of becoming, being, or remaining happy. They generally do not want someone else in control. But when non-binary sexual attraction enters the circle of family, friends, associates, or others with whom one is close, the picture often changes. The family, friends, and other acquaintances of the individual(s) with gender dysphoria may often become emotionally charged. Their earlier sensations of autonomy, freedom, and happiness evaporate rapidly because they see the transgender or transsexual as taking control. Yet a deeper introspection requires an analysis that discerns at exactly what, with whom, or some combination thereof, are they angry.

Initially, one may perhaps identify their transgender friend, associate, acquaintance, or loved one as the target of anger. Indeed, if they were not absorbed in that lifestyle, there would be no problem. But that is merely the surface cause of the situation. One might easily ask the individual, "Why have you let yourself be dragged into transgender identity?" "How could you not think of how this will destroy you, your future, and your testimony for the Lord Jesus, the One who died on the cross to pay the penalty for sin?" Further questioning might go something like this: "Why did you allow this to occur? Do you not know that you are the temple of the Holy Spirit?" The list could continue indefinitely until the person(s) begin to realize that this individual is a friend, family member, or perhaps even their own offspring. In time they note that their anger is projected elsewhere, such as toward people, technology, and other influences like the push-and-pull factors that initially prompted or enticed their acquaintance or loved one to enter the world of non-binary sexual expression. They often become angry at themselves and their relational skills for not establishing a solid foundation to protect against such out-side influences. They may cringe when overcome by influences such as the computer, internet, cell phones, social media, godless acquaintances, friends, colleagues, and perhaps relatives who tempted and encouraged their loved one down this dark path. Others may become angry because as they look back, they recall how their loved one, friend, or acquaintance spent so much time with certain people but could not really explain what they were doing. Some may at times remember how it seemed so strange that their friend or loved one spent so much time on the computer, not doing anything productive, or for how long they seemed to be communi-cating with others via technology rather than face-to-face. Many if not all of these and other thoughts will come, thankfully not simultaneously, but one by one they appear, and as they surface prompt anger to grow. It fre-quently begs the question especially among family, how could they have been so blind? How could this have been going on in their own home under their own roof? If relational transgender identity emerges with someone who dwells elsewhere, similar questions, slightly altered, often emerge. The result is the same, more anger, but it becomes increasingly directed at technology and other influences that resulted in the outcome they so dread. But anger is not done with them just yet.

Some may turn their wrath toward God. This is particularly true if the family has been active in the Lord's work. For instance, if parents brought up their child(ren) in the nurture and admonition of the Lord, it normally prompts them to presume that what their loved one was taught and presumably believed will continue throughout their lives. The Bible verses they memorized when younger will remain as an anchor in their lives, keeping them close to the Lord, facilitating a personal and intimate relationship with their Savior. Their potential rebellion seldom, if ever, enters into the picture. But when that behavior emerges it can become easy to blame God. They often pose queries to the Father such as, "God, how could you allow this to happen when parents, family, friends, and others were careful to provide and promote an evangelical environment? How could You allow them to experience such anguish and grief when they devoted so much of their lives and energy to You and Your work? Why are You punishing them through the dysphoria plaguing their loved one? How can they continue along this path of obedience when it appears that doing so will result only in continued distress and hopelessness?"

All these and other similar questions prompt awareness in their innermost being that grows until they finally begin to comprehend the true object of their anger. The evil one himself is behind it all. The apostle Paul described it perfectly in Ephesians 6:12: "For our struggle is not against flesh and blood, but against the rulers, against the powers, against the world forces of this darkness, against the spiritual forces of wickedness in the heavenly places." Their anger is ultimately directed toward Satan, as well as his army of demons who are out to destroy anything and anyone who stands for Christ. Family, friends, and others can finally aim their anger toward the liar, deceiver, and thief himself. Yet directing anger toward him does not solve anything. He is far bigger and more powerful than are humans and laughs at their miniscule outbursts. So, how do the angry come to terms with their emotion? Initially, it often seems to expand exponentially, but keep focused upon the Lord and His righteousness and remember that in time it will subside, and as it diminishes, the side effects will as well. Also at the end of the chapter, one may find helpful suggestions regarding this potentially explosive emotion.

A second sensation is guilt. Parents, family members, close friends, acquaintances, and others often develop a sense of responsibility for the situation in which they find themselves. Since they were the ones who had as much or more influence upon the transgender as anyone, it leads them to the sometimes erroneous conclusion that they are the cause. Something they did or did not do must have prompted their loved one to adopt transgender identity. They might examine some of their child-rearing techniques and strategies to see if perhaps they might have facilitated the situation. Siblings, cousins, friends, and associates may question their teasing, bantering, and other similar behaviors common in the transgender's early years. Along with that emotion surfaces the constant sense of wondering what others say or think about them and what went on in their family or their relationship during the child's formative years. Parents, siblings, and others often wonder what they did wrong. Their sense of responsibility has two elements; one is good while the other is not. The latter is perhaps better described as false guilt. This occurs when an individual has done nothing wrong but assumes responsibility for whatever may have occurred. Satan loves to execute this strategy to entrap believers and prompt them to grovel for forgiveness, and to make all sorts of promises to improve and not commit the same error again. Parents, family members, and others often fall into this trap, although they did not precipitate the situation in which they find themselves.

There is, however, another facet of responsibility which with the correct response can lead to quite positive results. If, for instance, a believer's actions, thoughts, ideas, or belief systems do not honor the Lord, they may detect a sense of personal wrongdoing. This is the Holy Spirit convicting that person of sin. There are undoubtedly times when a person's

God-dishonoring behavior is reflected by destructive decisions of close associates, children, friends, family, and others. Perhaps parents, colleagues, acquaintances, or others set a negative example, did not respond to certain stimuli in a Christlike manner, or they in some way or another failed in their position as a role model. This conviction comes from God and, when it results in a proper response by the guilty party—confession of that sin, repentance of that sin, and forsaking of that sin—brings them into a closer relationship with the Father.[16] In those situations, everyone would do well to abandon any hubris and confess their own personal error and sin not only to God but also to the family member who may have been wronged. The confessor does not need to, indeed should not, ask for the wronged party's forgiveness, because to do so will put the victim in an awkward situation. It essentially places the wronged person at the mercy of the sinner! It pressures them into forgiveness which they may or may not be ready to do. When and if the wronged individual is prepared to forgive, it will occur. Furthermore, one needs to be cognizant that often the one to whom they are confessing their wrongs may not want them to do so. If that is the case, ask them please to let the admission continue so the confessor may become relieved of its bondage. It will be cleansing for all and might even plant a seed in the individual with gender

---

[16] Confession means to agree with God that one has sinned and to tell Him its exact nature. Repentance is to experience remorse for the wrongdoing. It is precipitated by the Holy Spirit as He brings the sinner to an understanding of how s/he has transgressed against the Father and to turn completely away from it. Forsaking is to remove oneself completely from their rebellion. Thus, all three—confession, repentance, and forsaking—are essential components of maintaining a close, personal, intimate, and growing relationship with the Father.

dysphoria that perhaps they, too, may need to do the same. Indeed, one's primary objective should be to facilitate in their loved one or friend the need to pursue and develop a close, personal, intimate, and growing relationship with the Father. Therefore, the proper response to the conviction of personal sin can have fantastic outcomes. Granted, the results may not appear quickly, they may take years to materialize or perhaps not even occur in one's lifetime. But obedience to God and reacting to situations in a way that honors Him always prompts eternal blessings and rewards.

Just as Adam refused to admit his role in disobeying God but blamed Eve, sometimes family members, friends, and others follow a similar pattern. When transgender identity surfaces in a close relationship or family, chaos often ensues. Perhaps the husband blames his wife for being too gentle, too strict, too unorganized, or too perfectionistic. The wife, on the other hand, may blame her husband for being absent too much, too distant, too disinterested in their child's life, or too blunt and rough. Perhaps if siblings are involved, the parents may blame them, or vice versa. The same goes for friends and acquaintances. However one looks at it, the blame game, although popular, ignores the underlying issue. At best, it may allow for one person to let off steam, but at an incalculable and indefensible expense of another. In the final analysis, everyone needs to examine the question: how well did blaming, rather than confessing to the Lord, repenting and forsaking their sin and seeking God, serve Adam or Eve? They were required to accept the consequences both individually and corporately. Eve, among other things, had to experience great pain in childbirth, while Adam was forced to earn a living through difficult, painful, and challenging physical labor. Each was relocated from their Edenic paradise. Moreover, their personal relationship was undoubtedly damaged, and it most certainly did not speak well of their spiritual condition.

Whenever families face a major internal trial, it may result in relational havoc. It can, in fact, prompt a separation, divorce, disownment, or some other division primarily because everyone refuses to accept their potential role in the crisis. *Transitions of the Heart*, a book comprised of vignettes written by mothers of transgender and gender-variant children, may provide helpful insight. Georgia Myers noted that "parents should stand by their children no matter what life they choose to live." She continued to state that she "felt sorry for those families who do not accept, and even disown, their gay or transgender children. They are their own flesh and blood! Their children are human beings and have feelings." She concluded by urging "other parents to love their children unconditionally, no matter what."[17] The author did not discuss anything about a relationship with the Lord regarding herself or her child. This is unfortunate because the first and most important step in understanding one's identity is coming to terms with their relationship with Christ. There are only two options: either an individual is in Christ or is not; only those in Him can have an accurate comprehension of their true identity.

Families and others often refuse to seek help to process their emotions in a way that they believe brings honor to Christ. For instance, one may wish simply to leave and remove himself or herself from the situation, but how well does that work? At the very least, it may prompt more negative feelings within the transgender and does not point them to the Lord. It provides in no uncertain terms the clear and unmistakable message that the one who departs does not love the transgender and damages

---

[17] Rachel Pepper, ed. *Transitions of the Heart* (Berkeley, *Cleis Press*, 2012), 112, 100.

what is probably already a poor or fragile self-image. If nothing else, it clearly relates that the transgender is unwanted, unloved, unlovable, and definitely does not reflect the spirit of Christ. When people treat gender-variant family members, friends, associates, and others poorly, their testimony for Christ may be irreparably damaged, and it certainly reflects at best a stagnant and distant relationship with the Lord. How much wiser is the individual who, like Jesus in John 4, rejects a judgmental attitude and initiates a life-altering conversation with the woman at Jacob's well. She was undoubtedly familiar with disdain, having been married several times and currently living with a man, but Christ understood that she desperately needed compassion and understanding along with truth to lead her to Himself. Salvation, living in complete obedience to the Word as well as the indwelling Holy Spirit, and honoring the Father were the missing ingredients in her life. Therefore, those with transgender loved ones, family members, associates, and others would do well to minimize their focus on emotions, meditate on the wisdom of Solomon, and emulate the words and actions of Jesus.[18]

Those facing relational transgender identity or other situations that pierce to one's innermost being often indicate that they experience a long, deep, and treacherous valley through which the Lord guides them. Family members, friends, and others, for instance, need to recall that they influenced the transgender in the way that they believed was best. No reasonable person would, without cause, deliberately choose to do or not do anything that was contrary to their family member's or friend's best interest. Nevertheless, that piercing thought undoubtedly prompted the sensation David experienced that resulted in Psalm 23. The Hebrew

---

[18] John 4:1–42.

monarch was in a precarious and perhaps dangerous position, conceivably seeking refuge as a fugitive from King Saul or escaping from his rebellious son Absalom. Yet he trusted fully in the Lord's loving kindness. Therefore, respond as did Jesse's son, seek the Father's face and allow Him to use one's situation for His glory and for the edification of all. Permit the Lord to use the relational transgender identity and everything it entails to bring one into a closer relationship with Him. But as with anger, remember that Lucifer himself "prowls around like a roaring lion, seeking someone to devour." Do not provide him an opportunity to bring destruction.[19]

When focusing on emotions, all of which are inextricably intertwined with one another, it would be remiss not to include the next tormenting sensation. Anguish is perhaps the closest term to describe the mental, emotional, intellectual, and spiritual melee that emerges. Indeed, there truly is no word in the English language that accurately puts this into its proper perspective. Much like any parent who has not lost a child, or sibling who has not lost a brother or sister, cannot truly empathize with one who has, neither can a believer who has not experienced transgender identity among friends, acquaintances, or family fully commiserate with someone who has. Parents generally have a deep, unbreakable love for their child. Indeed, the Bible communicates in no uncertain terms that children are a blessing from the Lord. "Blessed is the man whose quiver is full...."[20] He normally permits parents the awesome privilege of rearing them. Furthermore, siblings, friends, and others make incalculable contributions to them as well. When one rejects their upbringing and the

---

[19]   1 Peter 5:8b.

[20]   Psalm 127:5a.

truths they learned, familial distress runs deep and friendships are greatly challenged. While in this compromised emotional state, Satan often hits hard with his most viscous lies, schemes, and deceit. He insinuates that the transgender's moms, dads, family members, friends, associates, and others demonstrated abysmal relational skills. He emphasizes any mistakes along with all the should-haves, could-haves, and would-haves but did-nots—although lacking any mention of the correct choices, the right and proper decisions, along with the positive contributions that typically far outweigh any negative influences. Satan can and undoubtedly does mislead parents and others into making rash, destructive, and un-Christlike decisions and prompts foolish behaviors which typically make a bad situation worse. It would, for example, not be unreasonable to learn of someone going as far as taking their own life to escape the emotional and mental torment and agony.

Yet as with the other emotions, this, too, will subside. The Lord Jesus sustains His children through this challenge as they rely on His Word, along with the Holy Spirit's direction, leadership, power, and compassion. The anguish will slowly diminish until it does not seem to comprise one's every waking moment. The Father wants believers to give Him the emotion. It is not His will for parents, family members, friends, and others to take responsibility for choices those close to them make. That is not to say that the evil one will not continue to harass and attack with his flaming missiles to wreak havoc and destruction. But, as Paul writes to the Ephesians, the Lord provides believers with protection from Lucifer, his minions, and their diabolical methods and strategies.

Shame is the fifth emotion that takes its heinous toll. It is important to note that it is closely associated with pride. With shame comes a sense of humiliation. Many dealing with familial transgender identity pose questions such as, "Should I tell anyone? What will my friends think? What about acquaintances I may see? How is this addressed in a Christmas letter? How will my extended family take this? How will my church handle this?" When we observe these and other related queries, it is not terribly difficult to discern the source, "Satan's flaming missiles." He truly enjoys taunting believers with questions that begin with "what if," "what will," and "what about." Thus, we know that these thoughts do not come from the Holy Spirit. Yet in their fallen state, people frequently tend to take responsibility for things that God never intended for them to bear. The Father's highest priority is for believers to have a close, personal, intimate, and growing relationship with Him. The wicked one will do what he can to prevent this from happening, so he works to realign people's focus from God to something or someone else. When one's attention is directed elsewhere, chaos enters. Think, for example, of the account in Matthew 14:28–30, when Peter climbed from his boat and began walking on water toward the Savior. The emboldened disciple bravely disembarked the vessel and started his trek. However, when he noticed the storm around him, fear hit and he began to sink. If believers maintain their focus on Christ they will not be distracted by the surrounding circumstances, nor will they be pulled into them. Satan, however, wants believers to focus on the periphery, away from the Father. Recall, however, God's promise in Isaiah 26:3–4: "The steadfast of mind You will keep in perfect peace, because he trusts in You. Trust in the Lord forever, for in God the Lord we have an everlasting Rock."

It is unrealistic to presume that all who encounter the challenge of transgender identity among friends, acquaintances, or family will experience only these emotions. An individual's personality and world-view as well as their walk with the Lord will have significant influence on what emotions emerge and the extent of their impact in one's life. Nevertheless, the Lord Himself provides all the resources necessary to prevent emotions from taking control and wreaking havoc with one's life. The apostle Paul, in his epistle to the Ephesians, explained in 6:10–17 that believers are in a spiritual war and Satan will do whatever he and his demons can to bring evangelicals to spiritual defeat. Indeed, he told Christians to "put on the full armor of God, so that you will be able to stand firm against the schemes of the Devil. For our struggle is not against flesh and blood, but against the rulers, against the powers, against the world forces of this darkness, against the spiritual forces of wickedness in the heavenly places."

What exactly is this armor and how can it help someone with their emotions and demonic attacks? Paul mentioned six specific pieces of armor: the girdle of truth, breastplate of righteousness, footwear, shield of faith, helmet of salvation, and finally the sword of the Spirit. A brief analysis illustrates clearly how to wear this armor and what it will do for a person's protection. Yet one must remember that the armor is only for a believer, one who has confessed, repented, and forsaken their sin and asked the Lord Jesus to enter their heart. It is only by His grace that sinners may receive salvation. It is also by grace through faith that they have access to the armor; thus, believers put it on by faith.

The girdle or belt of truth refers to a believer's identity in Christ. "Jesus said to him, 'I am the way and the truth and the life; no one comes to the Father but through me.'"[21] Moreover, in John 8:31–32, He stated,

---

[21]   John 14:6.

"If you continue in My word, then you are truly disciples of Mine; and you will know the truth and the truth will make you free." The Roman soldier's girdle kept all the armor in place and held the sword. To put on the belt, it is helpful to note several truths about believers. For example, they are saints, they are blessed with every spiritual blessing in the heavenly places, and they are holy and blameless before Him. Furthermore, believers are adopted, redeemed through His blood, and the recipients of His grace that He lavished upon them. Thanking the Lord for those and other specific truths about His own, such as the fact that their names are written permanently in the Lamb's Book of Life is how one puts on the girdle. Moreover, keep those things in mind throughout the day, much as the soldier wears the girdle all day. As Christians put on the belt daily it provides a proper and correct understanding of one's position in Christ. In time the accurate realization of who a believer is and what is their true identity becomes entrenched in both one's head and one's heart.

Secondly, put on the breastplate of righteousness. It is designed primarily to protect the heart, but other internal organs as well. It is essential for three purposes. First of all, it is to maintain one's devotion to God and God alone. Scripture communicates unmistakably that believers shall worship only Him and have no graven images. Therefore, ask the Father to reveal if and when anyone or anything comes between Him and oneself. Whatever or whomever the Holy Spirit reveals must go. A second intention is that believers need to confess any sin in their hearts, because they are the righteousness of Christ. "He made Him who knew no sin to be sin on our behalf, so that we might become the righteousness of God in Him."[22] If one harbors an unrepentant attitude, Satan has

---

[22] 2 Corinthians 5:21.

already asserted himself behind that crucial piece of armor and their personal defeat is assured. Thus, the protections provided by the Creator and Sustainer of the universe will prove ineffective. Finally, as a person's heart is safe, so are his or her emotions. People frequently respond to life's challenges emotionally rather than in the Spirit; when this happens, feelings run rampant, become out of control, and lead to disaster. Recall that God provided humans with emotions not to control their behavior, but to allow them to experience more fully the life with which they are blessed. When emotions remain under the power of the Holy Spirit, they allow people to sense heartache, happiness, disappointment, delight, and other feelings as well. When faced with an overwhelming situation, the breastplate of righteousness protects believers from acting out their sensations.

The third piece is the footwear. A Roman soldier wore a pair of *caligae*, which were heavy-duty leather sandals with extra thick soles embedded with spikes known as hobnails. The sandal, wrapped around the ankle, and sometimes up to the calf, provided a solid and steady foundation. When believers put these on, it is helpful to think of the spikes as giving them the ability to stand firm and not compromise the gospel of the Prince of Peace. Thank the Father that Christians are ambassadors of Christ, an instrument of His peace. Consistently walk in God's Will, always prepared to share the truth of salvation to those who need it. Visualize how His grace sustains His own as they do not water down the gospel or flee from encounters with Satan and his minions. Stand firm in the strength of His might.

Next the combatant takes up the shield of faith. It is a large, curved metal frame covered with thick leather, normally soaked in water. A soldier could hide behind the shield when under heavy attack from archers.

Scripture demonstrates explicitly that this piece of armor is designed to "extinguish the flaming arrows of the evil one." The ammunition is dipped in pitch and set on fire. The missiles are ideas, attitudes, perceptions, thoughts, and the like that the wicked one wants to plant in believers' minds. For instance, the notion that God does not really care about one's situation, if it feels good do it, no one will ever know if the behavior is hidden, everybody's doing it so join them, are but a few. Others may contain the message that they are terrible parents, family members, or friends, doing this just once will not cause problems. The list of wicked thoughts is continuous. To win this struggle, it is imperative that saints are aware of the fact that all kinds of evil ideas are sent their way by "the father of lies."[23] Paul's correspondence in Colossians 3:1–8, 16 explains in some detail how to protect one's mind. Indeed, by asking a few of the following questions, one will have a good idea of the thought's origin. "Where will this thought take me?" "Will these thoughts take me where I want to go?" "Are these thoughts biblically acceptable?" "Will these thoughts build me (or someone else) up or tear me (or another person) down?" "Do these thoughts show me as a follower of Jesus?" "May I share these thoughts with someone else?" "Do these thoughts prompt feelings of guilt?" One could clearly expand upon these queries and meditate upon the responses. By doing so, one is using the shield of faith effectively and protecting themselves and others from the wicked one's toxicity.[24] Thus, one must be on the lookout with their armor in place for anything that Satan sends their way. When soldiers know what ammunition is coming, they

---

[23] John 8:44b.

[24] Charles Stanley, "Taking Control of Your Thoughts" In Touch Ministries, 2015.

can be much better prepared. By utilizing the shield successfully, those wicked ideas, thoughts, and attitudes are extinguished and deflected. God knows Satan's operative strategies, so He provides the safety equipment for believers' protection. Picture someone in battle with arrows headed their way and they stand firm, holding out the shield to deflect the incoming ammunition. Thank the Lord for providing this armor.

Combatants then place on their heads the helmet of salvation. When one trusts Jesus as Lord and Savior, they receive the mind of Christ. Paul noted in Romans 12:2, "do not be conformed to this world, but be transformed by the renewing of your mind, so that you may prove what the will of God is, that which is good and acceptable and perfect." The Father wants Christians to develop His thinking patterns and thought processes to facilitate their spiritual growth, and to conform them to the image of His Son. Furthermore, believers are instructed in Colossians 3:1–2 that since "you have been raised up with Christ, keep seeking the things above, where Christ is, seated at the right hand of God. Set your mind on the things above, not on the things that are on earth." Paul noted to the Corinthians in his second letter that "though we walk in the flesh, we do not war according to the flesh, for the weapons of our warfare are not of the flesh, but divinely powerful for the destruction of fortresses." He continued, "We are destroying speculations and every lofty thing raised up against the knowledge of God, and we are taking every thought captive to the obedience of Christ,…"[25] An evangelical's walk with the Lord is in large part determined by what pervades his or her mind. If one thinks pure and holy thoughts and seeks the Father, their mind will be filled with Godly concepts and ideas. Thus, their conduct, conversation, and

---

[25]   2 Corinthians 10:3–5.

character reflect the Father. They will walk by grace and not likely succumb to the worldly nature and standards of right and wrong (or lack thereof) promoted by godless culture and society.

Finally, soldiers take up the sixth component of their uniform, the sword of the Spirit, which is the Word of God. It can be both defensive and offensive. First it is defensive, because if the wicked one's arrow manages to penetrate through the armor, the combatant can quote Scripture to Satan to reveal his deceitfulness. The sword is thus in some cases one's final line of defense. Believers need to learn to use it successfully. "Be diligent to present yourself approved to God as a workman who does not need to be ashamed, accurately handling the word of truth."[26] It is also an offensive weapon in that a person may become proactive rather than reactive. It is the means by which a soldier can move forward by defeating the enemy rather than simply waiting to be attacked. Yet using the sword effectively requires that believers know the Word. If one rarely opens the Scripture, seldom if ever meditates upon it, or perhaps knows only a handful of Bible passages, their sword will not be too useful. If studying Holy Writ and spending time with God are a low priority, combatants are defeated before the battle begins. Evangelicals must hide the Word in their hearts and allow it to permeate the depths of their very being. Believers are in a war with Satan. Note in Matthew 4 how Jesus, when tempted by Satan, used Scripture each time to defeat the wicked one. Christians have access to that same Word. If someone is serious about dealing with transgender identity, non-binary sexual expression, and other manifestations of wickedness among friends, acquaintances, or family, they must get to the point where they see that allowing their emotions and utilizing their

---

[26]   2 Timothy 2:15.

own strength will not succeed. Only through wearing and using the full armor of God are His own protected. Ask the Lord to bring His Word to memory and use it against Satan.

It is crucial that Christians dress with this armor each morning before getting out of bed. Daily visualize putting on each piece, recall what it does, acknowledge and thank the Lord for it. Remember that every component is essential. Full protection requires the entire armor of God. If something is missing, that is where the attack will come. Do this by faith and recall throughout the day that one is wearing it. Yet it is also important to pray earnestly that one is always receptive to the Spirit's leading. Sometimes the subtleties of the wicked one are so slight that one may not realize they are under siege. Therefore, remain on the alert for God's direction. When Satan begins to stir and one senses an attack, remind oneself of the armor and use it. Pick up the shield to deflect and extinguish the arrows, and think on things above where Christ is, seated at the right hand of God. Confess any sin, thank the Lord that He alone is worthy of worship, and give Him any emotions. Reflect upon one's ambassadorship for Christ, standing firm and refusing to compromise the gospel of His peace. Remember the reality of one's true identity in Christ and take up the Word of God. The Father provides freely these half-dozen pieces of armor: the girdle of truth, breastplate of righteousness, footwear, shield of faith, helmet of salvation, and finally the sword of the Spirit. Take and use them effectively.[27]

---

[27] For a fuller description of the battle armor, listen to Dr. Charles Stanley's message "Dressed for the Battle" that aired on *In Touch*, Friday, August 2, 2019, and August 5, 2019. See also D. Martyn Lloyd-Jones, *The Christian Soldier: An Exposition of Ephesians 6:10-13* 3rd printing. Grand Rapids: Baker Books, 2003 as well as Lloyd-Jones, *The*

CHAPTER 3

PHILOSOPHICAL, THEOLOGICAL, AND HISTORICAL FOUNDATIONS OF TRANSGENDER IDENTITY

"Therefore as you have received Christ Jesus the Lord, so walk in Him, having been firmly rooted and now being built up in Him and established in your faith, just as you were instructed, and overflowing with gratitude, see to it that no one takes you captive through philosophy and empty deception, according to the tradition of men, according to the elementary principles of the world, rather than according to Christ."

COLOSSIANS 2:6–8

Christian Soldier: An Exposition of Ephesians 6:10-20, Grand Rapids: Baker Books, 1983.

For believing families, friends, and others who grapple with transgender identity, transsexual identity, gender dysphoria, homosexuality and related phenomena, it may be helpful to examine briefly the philosophical roots of non-binary sexual expression. If they yearn for the fruit of the spirit such as love, joy, and peace among others to be produced and made evident in their lives, they must come to terms with the fact that biblically prohibited sexual expression is far broader than any one component of twenty-first century society or culture. The wicked one works to defeat Christians and set myriad traps, many of which are quite successful. Indeed, evangelicals often fall into Satan's deceptive snares of self-blame, questioning the Lord, and His sovereignty along with a host of other self-deprecating behaviors. Therefore, an examination of modern culture and its philosophical foundations is appropriate if not mandatory. Indeed, the undergirding perceptions of the sociocultural milieu determine in large part the direction that society moves. An understanding, even if cursory, helps people to comprehend more fully the broader picture of the times.

Satan schemes to get struggling saints to feel alone, that no one else can relate to their situation. He knows that discouragement becomes much stronger when believers sense that God deserted them. They may, for example, perceive themselves as abandoned in the middle of a gigantic desert, tired, thirsty, and famished with no oasis in sight. Every dune they cross takes them farther away from their intended destination. The sun beats mercilessly until it seems to become impossible to take one more step. Those hurting saints can truly relate emotionally to what Paul experienced physically as recorded in 2 Corinthians 1:8–9: "For we do not want you to be unaware brethren, of our affliction which came to us in Asia, that we were burdened excessively, beyond our strength, so that we despaired even of life; indeed, we had the sentence of death within ourselves so that we would not trust in ourselves, but in God who raises the dead;..." The Lord Jesus promised never to leave or forsake His own. Paul explained that believers are the temple of the Holy Spirit. The Greek word *naos*, translated temple in 1 Corinthians 3:16 and 6:19, actually refers to the Holy of Holies, the dwelling place of God in the tabernacle and later in the Jerusalem house of worship. Hence, Christians are, contrary to the wicked one's lie, never alone. Believers are not abandoned; rather, they are indwelt by God. Moreover, they are not the only ones facing what appears to be an impossible situation. Although it may be difficult to internalize because Satan's deceit is so subtle and effective, it is essential for evangelicals to accept and comprehend the notion that the social and cultural advancement and growing acceptance of transgender identity, transsexual identity, and gender dysphoria is considerably more extensive than they probably imagine. It is an issue much larger than any individual, family, or group. Although the phenomenon of non-binary sexual expression is rampant in culture and society, the numbers actually involved with it are minimal.

If a saint is to survive emotionally, spiritually, and intellectually intact the experience of familial or relational gender non-conformity, and assist others as they travel its arduous trail, a comprehension of the broader sociocultural and philosophical picture can be beneficial. It may enhance not only their success, but also their ability to sort things out cognitively, emotionally, as well as spiritually. Understanding Satanic strategies can prove invaluable as his targets cope with these and similar issues. A couple of biblical examples may prove helpful in this discussion. Holy Writ explains in Daniel 1:4–16 that if the exiles (Hebrews taken into captivity by the Babylonians) were to have a significant influence within Babylonian society, they needed to be well versed in the civilization's culture; notwithstanding the fact that much of it did not concur with Jewish belief, teaching, tradition, and understanding. Several young Hebrews were selected from among the captives to join Nebuchadnezzar's court. Daniel and his friends learned the language, literature, customs, philosophy, and other culturally relevant components of the Chaldean worldview. As part of their training, these young teenagers were also exposed to the culture's food and drink. Although surrounded by the king's delicacies, they refused to partake or imbibe and become defiled. Interestingly, after ten days of eating vegetables and drinking water, the young students were in better physical condition than were those who nourished themselves with the prime of Babylonian culinary delights.

Moreover, these exiles refused to allow the cultural surroundings to hinder their relationship with God. Think for instance of Shadrach, Meshach, and Abednego who would not worship Nebuchadnezzar's golden image and were tossed into his fiery furnace to fry. Daniel, who violated a treacherous edict banning prayer to anyone except Darius, was sentenced to spend a night in the den of lions. In both instances, all the men survived unscathed; they remained devoted solely to Jehovah. Believers are indwelt by the Holy Spirit who can and will empower them to do the same. Paul notes that "I can do all things through Him who strengthens me."[28] Indeed, the apostle writes in his second epistle to the Corinthians, "Therefore I am well content with weaknesses, with insults,

---

[28] Philippians 4:13.

with distresses, with persecutions, with difficulties, for Christ's sake; for when I am weak, then I am strong."[29]

A second example may be noted in 2 Timothy. The apostle Paul warned his protégé in the initial verses of chapter 3 that culture would deteriorate in the days ahead. In fact, later in that same correspondence, a heartbroken Paul noted that his once faithful co-laborer and companion Demas deserted him because he "loved this present world."[30] Although Christians dwell in a sin-tainted society, believers are not obligated to let it influence or determine their behaviors, attitudes, or beliefs. Nevertheless, many defend their non-biblical actions because of their surroundings or circumstances. Similarly, one can discern that culture played a negative role in the lives of numerous biblical characters. For instance, Demas allowed it to swallow him. In 1 Timothy 1:19–20, Paul encourages the pastor to maintain his "faith and a good conscience, which some have rejected and suffered shipwreck in regard to their faith. Among these are Hymenaeus and Alexander whom I have handed over to Satan, so that they will be taught not to blaspheme." Furthermore, Jannes, Jambres, Philetus, Korah, Diotrophes, and others chose popular culture over truth.[31] Nevertheless, Paul, Lydia, Ruth, Esther, Hannah, Judge Deborah, Luke, Mark, Timothy, Titus, and many others did not. Evangelicals, if they are to exert significant sociocultural influence, must find themselves among the faithful without regard to the cost. Indeed, a ship is safe on the ocean as long as

---

[29] 2 Corinthians 12:10.

[30] 2 Timothy 4:10.

[31] See, for instance, 2 Timothy 2:16–18; Exodus 7:10–13; 2 Timothy 3:8–9; Numbers 16; and 3 John 9–11.

the ocean is not in the ship. But once water enters the vessel, it is in serious trouble. When believers allow the sociocultural influences, no matter how strong or enticing, to distract them, disaster approaches rapidly.

This chapter is in no way intended to relay all significant theological, philosophical, and cultural components of America in the early decades of the twenty-first century. It is, however, designed to facilitate a basic understanding of what is occurring, why it is happening, and how the transgender, transsexual, sexual non-conforming, and other non-binary sexual movements emerged. Current sociocultural conditions are briefly surveyed through two basic perspectives: the first is via the broad concept of modernism that may be applied to Western culture in general. Secondly, the piece surveys a specifically American approach that encompasses theological, social, political, and historical consequences of the seismic philosophical changes of the past several centuries. While reading this chapter, keep in mind that its principal objective is to demonstrate how a preponderance of the nation's theologians, philosophers, and sociocultural warriors have over time established a society and culture that has become close to accepting non-binary sexual expression as not abnormal. America's current sociocultural position is not something that started three, six, or nine decades ago. Rather it has, in many respects, been developing since the early European colonization of North America; thus, it is well entrenched, and far larger and more influential than any individual, sociocultural issue, or generation.

Whether cognizant of it or not, every person with the ability to reason has a comprehensive conception or perspective of the universe; all have perceptions of their specific realm. A person's worldview includes but is not limited to ideas regarding the creation, foundation, or formation of the universe. Is there a purpose of, reason for, or meaning of, human life? If so, what is it? If not, why are humans on earth? Is there a relationship between the universe and humanity? If so, what is it? Is there some force or being around which life, the world, and universal events revolve, or does perhaps everything occur by chance? What exactly is physical death? Is there an existence of life after physiological demise occurs? If so, what is its form? These questions are asked in a simplistic manner requiring an uncomplicated response. Clearly, one's actual queries are far more sophisticated. But it is apparent that the answers one provides tend to indicate his or her worldview. As an example, one may adopt a biblical or Christocentric worldview which maintains that God as revealed through Scripture is the very core of creation, life, and the questions are answered accordingly. Contrariwise, one may take a naturalistic or perhaps materialistic approach which does not allow for the existence of a spiritual realm. Humans have no eternal component but are solely material or physical. At death their existence ceases. They tend to accept an evolutionary explanation for the universe's beginning, development, and perhaps eventual extinction. These are but two examples of many worldviews. Whichever outlook a person adheres to will strongly influence their attitude regarding sexual non-conformity.

Another way to describe this is that every person who can think rationally and comprehend logically has ideas or conceptions of the universe. These notions are swayed heavily by their intellectual, emotional, and philosophical understanding of life. If, say, someone wears glasses with a red-colored tint, they will perceive the world with that same hue. If another person uses cerulean or azure spectacles, they visualize surroundings in blue; if yet a third has yellow and a fourth green, their perspectives are tinted with those colors. Remember, all witness the same world, but their mind's interpretation (the colored glasses) will determine how it is perceived and understood. The lens through which one views and understands the world is the rough equivalent of their worldview. It, in turn, is often heavily impacted by their surrounding culture and society. Hence, as civilizations, societies, cultures, and philosophies emerge, progress, and alter through the centuries, so too do people's widespread popular perceptions. This does not in any way state, infer, or even imply that all agree with their culture's general perspective, because many do not. It does, however, in the most basic manner, describe how cultural and social comprehensions of issues such as sexual expression can and do modify. A person's worldview or colored lens will have a significant impact in the way in which they view non-binary sexual expression.

During the previous thousand years or so, predominant philosophical trends may generally be divided into three chronological phases of development: premodernism, modernism, and postmodernism.[32] To maintain a sense of brevity, this piece examines only a minuscule component of Western philosophy, the study of knowledge. Epistemology encompasses issues such as the source, validity, reliability, veracity, and extent of knowledge. Primarily, attention is given to absolute truth, the

---

[32] Utilizing dates and separating basic Western philosophy into general categories can and often does oversimplify complex subjects. Indeed, some disagree with using terms such as premodernism, modernism, or postmodernism as they are extremely broad and tend to impose current understanding on the past. They are employed here merely as a means of convenience to define and describe trends and developments as they regard non-conforming gender and sexual expression within a historical context to a contemporary audience.

concept that something is true and accurate without respect to time, place, culture, society, or any other potential limitation. Relativism, on the other hand, contends that a specific culture or society at a certain time may hold something to be true, but that same thing may be unacceptable at a different time in another sociocultural setting.

During the time when premodernism held sway across Western Europe, the source of truth was God, especially as He was defined by the predominant Catholic Church. Nevertheless, pockets of believers who rejected the overwhelming influence of Roman Catholicism lived during that era as well.[33] They understood God essentially as He was revealed through Scripture. It was not a truth that could be proven but rather came to an individual via disclosure from the Holy Spirit in conjunction with the Word. One could not perform some type of experiment and prove or disprove God's existence. It was simply attained by reading and meditating on Scripture and sensing the Holy Spirit's revelation of truth. One component of absolute truth was binary sexuality. Women were women and men were men.

By the mid to late seventeenth century, a new philosophical movement emerged that fostered significant change within the discipline of epistemology. Many influential people helped precipitate this change. Yet we will examine briefly only two noted thinkers often associated with the emergence of modernism. The first was John Locke, a physician, political

---

[33] A few of these groups included the Waldensians, Anabaptists, and Lollards. For more information see Williston Walker, Richard A Norris, David W. Lotz and Robert T. Handly *A History ot the Christian Church* 4th *ed., (MacMillan Publishing Company: New York), 1985;* and Earl E. Cairnes, *Christianity Through the Centuries: A History of the Christian Church,* (Zondervan Publishing House, Grand Rapids), 1981.

philosopher, and author. He rejected the notion of accepting absolute truth by means of direct revelation. Rather, he promoted the concept known as empiricism. For instance, he contended that all babies were born *tabula rasa* or blank slate. Every component of that individual's persona emerged as a direct result of their sensory experiences. Furthermore, he argued for the use of empirical information. In essence, for something to be accepted as true, it needed to be proven with evidentiary material. Since there was no way to substantiate undeniably God's existence, it could not be accepted uncritically.

The second noted individual was Rene Descartes. He argued for the precept known as rationalism. In his mind, reason was the bottom line for what was and was not true. Belief in God or anything supernatural was, according to Descartes, illogical; therefore, it could not be accepted without question. Indeed, he is perhaps best known for the quote "I think, therefore I am." An individual with the ability to think, or rationalize, provides sufficient evidence to prove their existence. Thus, with modernism, direct revelation gave way to empiricism and rationalism. Although it does not preclude the concept of absolute truth, modernism does raise some serious concerns regarding its veracity. The ideas of God's existence as well as binary sexuality lost their stance as absolute. In other words, Western culture made a huge leap away from its foundation upon Scripture, and truth became much more culturally relative. It could change according to time, culture, and society, opening the door for non-biblical sexual expression.

Some three centuries subsequent, postmodernism emerges as a growing philosophical position, and by the second millennium, it clearly holds sway. Unlike with the modern era, one cannot distinguish any particular philosophers as its founders but rather to a gradually developing mind-set of accepting various means by which knowledge may be attained. Postmodernists argue, among other things, that knowledge is subjective rather than objective. What is true for one culture or society is not nec-essarily accepted by another. Indeed, nearly all postmodernists reject the idea of Scripture being the final authority. Those who argue for the legit-imacy of absolute truth are often relegated by cultural elites to the fringe element of society. Biblical inerrancy and infallibility are rejected. It was composed by too many persons over too long a time, involved too many cultures too many years ago to maintain validity. Hence, the dominant worldview is far removed from biblical admonitions.[34] The binary sexual reality of man and woman is no longer absolute but merely one of a host of options regarding sexual expression.

Slowly but steadily, the world's dominant philosophical under-standing regressed from a scriptural foundation to one based on human thought and logic. Thus, one can discern how something completely unthinkable during the premodern era becomes accepted and encouraged with postmodern philosophy. Western culture and American society are

---

[34] D. A. Carson, *The Gagging of God: Christianity Confronts Pluralism* (Zondervan: Grand Rapids, 1996. ePub ed. 2009). Please note that the term postmodernism is controversial in and of itself. Because it is so broad, many refuse to use it. For a scholarly study, see Nicholas C. Burbules, "Postmodernism and Education," Jan 2010 DOI: 10.1093/oxfordhb/9780195312881.003.0029 (accessed November 7, 2019) in Harvey Seigel, ed. The Oxford Handbook of Philosophy of Education (Oxford: Oxford University Press, 2010). DOI: 10.1093/oxfordhb/9780195312881.001.0001 (accessed November 7, 2019).

permeated with a relativistic mindset that changes according to society, culture, and time.[35]

Theological ideas and perspectives have a significant and unmistakable influence upon a nation's mindset. Two scriptural examples illustrate the point. During the biblical period of the Judges, the Hebrews worshipped Jehovah when a God-honoring woman or man such as Deborah or Gideon ruled. The Lord brought military success or peace. But following that individual's death, the people soon turned away and praised the deities of indigenous people. The Hebrews quickly fell under the tyranny of a pagan society. Fast-forward several hundred years to the time of the kings which began with Saul and David. Subsequent to the latter's death, the nation of Israel's culture, society, and actions were largely contingent upon the king's relationship with and obedience to God. When he led the people to worship and obey Jehovah, they flourished, but when the opposite occurred, the nation moved away from the Lord until godlessness and immorality pervaded the people and their enemies held sway. America is no different. An insightful monograph authored by the late historian C. Gregg Singer provides a historical framework through which readers may view and understand how American philosophical and theological movements in particular have influenced the nation's sociocultural perspective. How could something that was once considered unthinkable, non-binary sexual expression, become by many, accepted and encouraged behavior?

Without question, the initial theological philosophy that permeated what became America was Puritanism. In the early seventeenth century when they appeared in New England, Puritans planned to create a "City

---

[35] For a fuller discussion, see Gene Edward Veith, Jr., *Postmodern Times: A Christian Guide to Contemporary Thought and Culture* (Wheaton: Crossway Books, 1994).

on a Hill" for all to see how they could live successful and productive God-honoring lives.[36] The concept of God's sovereignty permeated virtually every decision they made. Each component of their culture was based on the Bible, the whole counsel of God. The widespread influence of these early colonists initiated in the American psyche a kingdom of God. The primary responsibility of government was to enforce the laws, most of which were based chiefly upon Scripture.[37]

However, by the latter half of the seventeenth century, problems emerged. Descendants of the initial settlers did not maintain their ancestor's vim and vigor. Theology became less biblical and more humanistic. Doctrines such as original sin and total depravity lost much influence, while scientific discoveries, philosophical treatises such as the social contract, and new technologies emerged. All of which prompted a move away from the original culture based solely on Holy Writ. Absolute truth regarding sexuality, among other things, was in the early stages of decline.

Deism emerged later in the seventeenth century. Its formulators had many questions about epistemology. They argued, for example, that Christianity placed far too much emphasis on God, especially as revealed through Scripture, as the primary source of knowledge. Rationalism, many contended, was a much more reliable source of truth. Rene Descartes and other "Enlightenment" thinkers continued to acknowledge the existence of God as Creator but rejected the idea that He did anything else. John

---

[36] For a fuller discussion of the Puritans, see Edmund S. Morgan, *The Puritan Dilemma, The Story of John Winthrop, 3rd ed.* Mark C. Carnes, ed. (Hoboken: Pearson, 2006).

[37] C. Gregg Singer, *A Theological Interpretation of American History,* Rev. ed. (Solid Ground Christian Books: Vestavia, AL, 2009), 10–15.

Locke, one of deism's most popular and influential apologists, argued for empiricism. In time, his political philosophy gained significant support.[38]

Deism's popularity, however, was short-lived. By the 1820s or so, it was losing favor as the preeminent religious/philosophical/political system in America. A new dogma, transcendentalism, soon entered the picture. It was expounded by noted notables such as Ralph Waldo Emerson, Henry David Thoreau, Louisa May Alcott, and others who advanced personal individualism and autonomy. Transcendentalists tended to accept the innate goodness of people, but humanity's original purity was polluted not through a sinful nature but by organized religion along with political parties. They viewed those institutions as hindering self-reliance while promoting dependence.[39]

They embraced a more spiritual approach to life, not in the Christian sense, but more like animism (the notion that spirits indwell objects of nature). A chief objective of the transcendentalist was to become one with her or his natural surroundings. Unlike the previous philosophical or theological movements, transcendentalism rejected the concept of absolute truth, be it Scripture, rationalism, or perhaps even binary sexuality. Truth, no longer considered absolute, became relative to culture or society. Religion became merely a form of piety with moralism as its chief

---

[38] Eric Foner, *Give Me Liberty: An American History, 4th Brief Ed. Vol. 1* (New York: W.W. Norton, 2012), 124–27, 172–75.

[39] For a more extensive list of authors, publications, and influences, see American Transcendentalism Web: www.vcu.edu/engweb/transcendentalism/index.html.

objective. It essentially removed the Father, the Son, and the Holy Spirit and adopted humanism.[40]

Following the Civil War, the economic boom that affected the North needed a philosophy to justify its expansion.[41] Hence, later in the nineteenth century, Social Darwinism appeared. Herbert Spencer applied the notion of Darwin's survival of the fittest to Western social and cultural systems. He contended that the laws of nature determined how society functioned. For instance, he and his adherents viewed Christianity as promoting the feeble in that it required dependence upon Christ for one's personal salvation. Along with Social Darwinism emerged the notion of pragmatism. John Dewey argued that if an idea (such as personal salvation) or invention has no functional value, it will cease. Hence, one can see the continual diminishing credibility that American social and intellectual leaders held for the basic tenets of Christianity. If, for instance, sexual conformity does not seem to function, experiment with non-binary sexual expression. Each philosophical step moved the nation farther away from truth that is absolute toward that which is relative to culture or society. Nevertheless, some cultural Christians were concerned about the drifting of American society, so several ushered in a new movement which ultimately exacerbated the move away from the Lord.[42]

---

[40] Singer, *A Theological Interpretation*, pp. 56–64.

[41] See Harold Livesay *Andrew Carnegie and the Rise of Big Business*, 3rd ed. Mark C. Carnes, ed. Hoboken: Pearson, 2007.

[42] Singer, *A Theological Interpretation*, 126–27. For perhaps the best classical analysis of Social Darwinism in America, see Richard Hofstadter, *Social Darwinism in American Thought*. Boston: Beacon Press, 1992.

The Social Gospel entered America with the onset of Social Darwinism. A number of noted clergymen such as Henry Ward Beecher, Henry Drummond, and Lyman Abbott applied Darwin's tenets to Christianity. Society was improving and the church should do what it could to alleviate suffering but not concern itself with an individual's relationship with the Father. Thus, the move from the Triune God continued unabated. Rather than worship the Creator and Sustainer of the universe, many instead offered adoration to the creation. In lieu of absolute truth was social and cultural reality. As the nation moved away from the Oneness of the Father, the Son, and the Holy Spirit, America moved closer to the philosophical and religious concept of pluralism. In many respects, America had in a religious sense reverted back to the time of the Judges when Scripture states in 21:25, "In those days there was no king in Israel; everyone did what was right in his own eyes."

Theological liberalism (the concept that Scripture is essentially irrelevant) came into its own in the 1920s and continued the nation down its dark path. By that time, the anti-evangelical or pluralistic perspective garnered support from most intellectuals and academicians, even those who claimed to be Christian. Soon they controlled denominational colleges, seminaries, and other institutions of higher learning. Salvation by grace through an individual's personal faith in the shed blood of Christ was no longer preached; instead, topics of Sunday discourses were chiefly salvation by a perfected society, various reform movements, and a culture permeated by scientific inquiry.[43]

The global economic disaster which had been fomenting since the

---

43   Edwin Scott Gaustad, *A Religious History of America New Revised Ed.* (San Francisco: Harper, 1990), 261–280. Note also Pluralism and Unity: www.expo98.msu.edu/.

end of World War I attracted universal attention in 1929 with the stock market crash. Most focused on the temporary crisis rather than eternal truth. Biblically ordained sexual expression continued to lose influence. Pragmatism again surfaced as a primary baseline, providing even less credence to absolute truth, the basic foundation of Western civilization.[44] Following World War II, theological liberals had even more material for their crusade against biblical truth. They viewed the war as God's mistake because He did not prevent the nations from taking up arms against each other. He also permitted the Holocaust along with the deaths of tens of millions who perished in the strife. If God could err in allowing destructive worldwide conflicts and unspeakable atrocities, He could certainly make an incorrect determination of one's birth sex. During the nearly three-quarters of a century since the Axis Powers surrendered to the Allies, America has continued on the path away from Biblicism toward secularism. Humanistic pluralism, sociocultural relativism, and pragmatism replaced the Lord and Scripture as the center of culture, society, theology, morality, and beliefs. Indeed, the United States and much of the world are clear examples of what the prophet Isaiah wrote: "'For My thoughts are not your thoughts Nor are your ways My ways,' declares the Lord. 'For as the heavens are higher than the earth, so are My ways higher than your ways and My thoughts than your thoughts.'" Also one may read in Proverbs: "There is a way which seems right to a man, but its end is the way of death."[45]

Therefore, Americans today have a culture which, over the course

---

[44] Singer, *A Theological Interpretation,* 226–32.

[45] Gaustad, *Religious History of America,* 280–379; Isaiah 55:8–9; Proverbs 14:12.

of a few centuries, abandoned the influential Puritan view of Scripture, the sovereignty of God, as well as salvation by grace through faith in the atoning sacrifice of the Lord Jesus. It is now humanistic to its very core and worships the trinity of pluralism, pragmatism, and cultural relativism. Humans and their feelings, or perhaps even experiences, rather than God, become the measure of all things. If one feels like a woman although born a man, their sensory perception takes precedence over biological reality. Contrariwise, if one is born a woman but feels like a man, who is anyone to question that person's reality even if it opposes all organic (physical) evidence? Because one feels more at home in a sex different from what that individual was born, society and culture become obligated to insure that the person is affirmed into the sex with which they are more comfortable.

Thus, it becomes apparent that transgender identity is made philosophically, theologically, and religiously tenable by the slow but steady removal of God and Scripture as the foundation of American culture and society. Human thinking and sociocultural relativism replaced absolute truth with cultural veracity. Hence truth can vary from one culture or society to another. God, His righteousness, holiness, sovereignty, and unchanging truth are all rejected as irrelevant, and the world continues down its rebellious path that began in the Garden of Eden.

CHAPTER 4

SCIENTIFIC EVIDENCE REGARDING GENDER DYSPHORIA, TRANSGENDER IDENTITY, AND TRANSSEXUAL IDENTITY

"Lift up your eyes on high and see who has created these stars, the One who leads forth their host by number, He calls them all by name; because of the greatness of His might and the strength of His power not one of them is missing." Why do you say, O Jacob, and assert, O Israel, "My way is hidden from the Lord, and the justice due me escapes the notice of my God?" Do you not know? Have you not heard? The Everlasting God, the Lord, the Creator of the ends of the earth does not become weary or tired.

His understanding is inscrutable.

ISAIAH 40:26–28

As transgender identity gains traction in its sweep across America, numerous arguments propose that it is a biological rather than a psychiatric, psychological, emotional, or perhaps even a spiritual issue. A brief synopsis concerning the history of diagnostic analyses of psychiatric and psychological disorders demonstrates that we are dealing with the manifestation of a long-brewing tendency regarding mental health diagnoses. In the early twentieth century, several mental health organizations along with the federal government compiled the first manual dedicated to mental health maladies. It was published under various names in numerous editions until the *Diagnostic and Statistical Manual of Mental Disorders* (DSM) came into existence in 1952. The overriding presupposition of these publications and the organizations that published them was that mental disorders were brought on by various causalities, the vast majority of which were inorganic. Perhaps because of societal upheavals of the 1960s, along with the low regard that the public and many in the medical community held for psychiatry and psychology, various influential practitioners schemed to alter the basic premise of psychiatry from a causality or psychodynamic approach to empiricism or sensory experience. In other words, the notion of one's environment, upbringing, or other non-biological origin was in large part replaced by a biological foundation. A person's genetic, instinctive, inborn traits became far more influential than their familial background, social surroundings, or environmental circumstances.[46]

This altered perspective prompted no fewer than two major

---

[46] Shadia Kawa and James Giordano, "A Brief Historicity of the DSM: Issues and implications for the future of psychiatric canon and practice," *Philosophy, Ethics and Humanities in Medicine,* January 13, 2012; 7:2 doi:10.1186/1747-5341-7-2.

consequences for the general public and their relationship with mental health treatment. First is that society and its perceptions became a crucial component in the definition of a disorder as well as its diagnosis and treatment. For instance, the public, the American Psychiatric Association (APA), or the American Psychological Association (also noted by the abbreviation APA) might determine that a disorder which for centuries was considered abnormal or highly atypical should no longer be regarded within that context. The condition, following a few formalities, is no longer considered a treatable syndrome and becomes "normal." What were defined as taboos from the origins of Western civilization emerge as acceptable. Homosexuality is a case in point. What since the time of Abraham, Moses, and the Judges was regarded as an abomination and sin by many and later a mental illness by others was, in 1973, due in large part to social and other homosexual interest group pressures, removed by the APA as a mental illness and not included in the DSM-III, published in 1980.[47]

Encouraged in large part by influential homosexuals within the

---

[47] Considerable evidence suggests that homosexuality was not uncommon among the ancient Greeks and Romans. Indeed, Paul condemns the behavior numerous times in his scriptural correspondence, so one may reasonably presume that it was a frequent component of societies and cultures with which he was familiar. Yet it also occurred much earlier. For example, the account of Sodom and Gomorrah, which were both closely associated with same-sex activities, occurred during Abraham's lifetime in perhaps the 2000s B.C. Moses, who authored the Hebrew Law, probably lived during the 1400s B.C. The book of Judges describes the bloody Benjamite War. It occurred in about 1200 B.C. and was precipitated in part by a defense of homosexual behavior. In each biblical account, it is regarded as an egregious sin to be expunged. For more information, see Genesis 18–19, Leviticus 18–20, and Judges 19–21.

APA and elsewhere, what was once addressed with relative success through reparative therapy suddenly became something counselors were instructed not to treat. Indeed, it became illegal in certain circumstances. Rather than seeking to provide some relief to those wanting to abandon the homosexual lifestyle, therapists were delegated to encourage clients who suffered with a sexual abnormality to "accept" it as their lot in life. There was nothing they could do to change it. They were doomed to live with their mental and sexual incongruence. The transgender movement became strikingly similar to the homosexual conduit. It became "normal-ized" by powerful leaders within the APA. Gender identity disorder was rechristened gender dysphoria and essentially morphed into a nebulous state, including but not limited to transgender identity, transsexual identity, non-binary sexual expression, and gender fluidity.

Secondly, if a psychological or psychiatric disorder is regarded as biological in nature, the presumption becomes that the condition is not deemed abnormal in a psychological or psychiatric sense. Hence, there should be no attempt to approach the issue through counseling and/or psychiatric medication therapy. Nevertheless, extensive evidence strongly suggests that non-binary sexual attraction and behavior may be altered when the individual with that mindset wants and is prepared to change and mental health professionals or other resource persons are asked to assist in the process.

For example, Alan Finch, a nineteen-year-old Australian man, tran-sitioned to Helen Finch, but a decade and a half subsequent contended that "You can't fundamentally change sex...." He continued, "The surgery doesn't alter you genetically. It's genital mutilation." Finch commented further, "The fact that someone's suicidal and wanting something isn't a reason to provide it. The analogy I use about giving surgery to someone desperate to change sex is it's a bit like offering liposuction to an anorexic." Because of his eye and mind-opening experiences, "Finch helped to set up the Gender Identity Awareness Association, to dissuade people from genital surgery and campaign against what he calls the "sex change industry." Since then, "Finch's outreach website has been archived and there is no further information online. In fact, Finch's subsequent silence is the norm for those who change their minds."[48]

Matthew Attonley underwent the "gender affirmation surgery" at twenty-three, but within seven years made arrangements to abandon "Chelsea" and return to his natural birth sex. If transgender identity or transsexual identity had an organic causation, why do these and countless others, who requested to be corrected to their mentally proper sex, regret the change and often pursue opportunities to be altered back to their birth sex? This makes no sense if one understands it as an organic issue, but becomes much more logical when viewed as an inorganic phenomenon.[49]

Much of the remaining portion of this chapter explores two trends in modern psychiatry and psychology. One is the tendency to focus on biological etiology rather than psychological or psychiatric causality, while the other is the growing acceptance of social, cultural, and personal perceptions regarding what does and does not necessitate treatment. Today, nearly anyone who views a non-binary sexual condition as abnormal or

---

[48] David Batty, "Mistaken Identity," *The Guardian, US Edition*, July 30, 2004; Stella Morabito, "Trouble in Transtopia: Murmurs of Sex Change Regret," *The Federalist*, November 11, 2014.

[49] Selwyn Duke, "The Transgender Con? Many 'Transgender' People Regret Switch," *The New American*, November 11, 2014, republished 2017.

sinful is rebuffed by mainstream culture and society, notwithstanding the fact that scientists have yet to identify any biological etiology or cause. There is no homosexual prompting gene. In October 2015, Dr. Tuck Ngun garnered considerable attention from his study on 37 pairs of identical male twins when he presented his research titled "Epigenetic Algorithm Accurately Predicts Male Sexual Orientation" at the American Society of Human Genetics. The presentation from his defective project resulted in highly deceptive headlines such as "Have They Found the Gay Gene?" in London's October 9, 2015, edition of *Metro*, and in the October 8, 2015, *Los Angeles Times* "Scientists find DNA differences between gay men and their straight twin brothers." Even *New Scientist* ran a disingenuous title, "Gay or straight? Saliva test can predict male sexual orientation."[50] However, a more insightful and accurate Ed Yong, science writer for *The Atlantic,* noted on October 10, 2015, "No, Scientists have not Found the 'Gay Gene.'" He noted, among other things, that the study was minis- cule at best and the chemical markers he used tainted the results. "So," according to Yong, "what we have is an underpowered fishing expedition that used inappropriate statistics and that snagged results which may be false positives."[51] His unreliable study prompted dishonest results, which were then given a misleading and erroneous interpretation. All of which was used by the mainstream media to promote their biased and unsup- ported agenda. Moreover, it is helpful to understand that Ngun himself is homosexual and active in the LGBTQ community. Also, one of his chief

---

[50] Jessica Hamzelou, "Gay or straight? Saliva test can predict male sexual orientation" *New Scientist*, October 8, 2015.

[51] Ed Yong, "No, Scientists have not found the 'gay gene,'" *The Atlantic*, October 10, 2015.

apologists, David Geffen, is a wealthy gay philanthropist who donates substantially to the LGBTQ cause and to the University of California at Los Angeles, Ngun's employer as well as the location of his project. In fact, their school of medicine is named for Geffen.

Nearly a year prior to that study, Kenneth Kendler, a psychiatric geneticist at Virginia Commonwealth University, stated that "no one believes that a single gene or genes can make a person gay. Any genetic predispositions probably interact with environmental factors that influence development of a sexual orientation."[52] Kendler's assessment probably best sums the mainstream position; a specific organic cause cannot be determined (but they presume it is present), so it is included along with inorganic criteria. There may be some environmental causes, but it is essentially biological so the choice of becoming homosexual is removed. However, the historical data regarding homosexuality has not changed; rather it has been reinterpreted chiefly upon the basis of various current social, psychological, psychiatric, and cultural trends. Perhaps this prompted New Scientist to print the salacious article "Gay Gene Discovery Has Good and Bad Consequences." The piece concludes "what causes homosexuality doesn't matter as much as the fact that homosexual people exist, and have always existed, in every society on earth. In the words of the activists: Some people are gay. Get over it."[53]

There are far fewer scientific studies available on transgender identity

---

[52] Kelly Servick, "Study of Gay Brothers may confirm X chromosome link to homosexuality," Science, November 17, 2014.

[53] New Scientist, "Gay gene discovery has good and bad implications." https://www.newscientist.com/article/mg22429963-700-gay-gene-discovery-has-good-and-bad-implications/#ixzz60l6QlynI.

and transsexual identity, but those accessible for consideration produce similar results. No, there is (are) no specific gene, genes, or combination thereof that can pinpoint a biological etiology. The late noted sexologist Richard Green profoundly influenced the examination of transgender identity in psychology. His seminal work *Sexual Identity Conflict in Children and Adults* prompted the inclusion of gender identity disorder as a mental diagnosis in DSM-III published in 1980. Green attempted to combine the biological and psychological causes when he spoke on the question of whether transsexuals had that orientation from conception. He suggested that the answer is yes, but his reasoning was based on the following considerations. First, transsexuals had more maternal aunts than uncles, and second, male transsexuals had more older brothers than average.[54] Dissecting these two arguments is not excessively challenging in that the transsexual's aunts would probably have been born prior to the child's conception, so how could that in itself have any influence? What is perhaps more important, but deliberately unexamined, is the relationship between the transsexual and the maternal aunts. Regarding the second argument, the transsexual's brothers would also have been born prior to the transsexual's conception. Therefore, just as with the aunts, the transsexual's relationship with their brothers is certainly a plausible but unexplored cause. Moreover, birth-order studies have long confirmed that placement within a family can indeed have a huge influence upon a person's development, sexual and otherwise. During the early decades of the twentieth century, Viennese psychiatrist Alfred Adler wrote and spoke extensively

---

[54] Richard Green, "Is Being Transgender Genetically Determined at Conception?" Address delivered to the Ontario Consultants on Religious Tolerance, December 18, 2017.

on the topic. He contended that character traits and individual behaviors depended largely on developmental issues such as birth order, among a host of other influences. Succeeding scholars have developed this theory further. For instance, Alan E. Stewart authored *Adlerian Psychotherapy* in 2002 and Kevin Leman produced *The Birth Order Book* two decades previous. Thus, these two ideas from Green provide considerably more evidence for the position that transgender identity and transsexual identity is determined after birth rather than before. Inorganic rather than organic causation becomes much more probable.

If a psychological or psychiatric disorder is regarded as biological in nature, then the presumption becomes that the condition is not deemed mentally or emotionally abnormal. It is removed from a treatable diagnosis to one that needs to be accepted, approved, and even encouraged. Hence, we see the rise of transgender identity, transsexual identity, and other examples of gender non-conformity. A transgender, transsexual, gender non-conformist, or a host of others can thus say, "I was born this way. There was no choice on my part." Yet another mantra of the transgender crowd says, "With the discrimination they face, why would anyone choose to be transgender?" "There is nothing I can do to change myself." It is in essence removing the scriptural definition as sin and rebellion and replacing it with what society is pressured into believing as perfectly acceptable behavior. The situation is not far removed from the accurate but discerning words penned by the prophet Jeremiah in 2:13: "My people have committed two evils; they have forsaken Me, the fountain of living waters, to hew for themselves cisterns, broken cisterns that can hold no water." Hence, we see the Father's perspective eliminated as the primary point of reference regarding human sexuality. It is replaced with the view approved by mainstream Western society and culture. Furthermore, numerous academicians, scientists, and others search tirelessly in their quest to locate some specific organic cause. As with homosexuality, those who do not embrace transgender identity, transsexual identity, gender dysphoria, gender fluidity, or a host of other non-traditional views of binary sexuality are often subject to public ridicule, loss of employment opportunities, and even highly serious legal action.[55]

If one can conclusively corroborate that nature is primarily responsible for all non-conforming sexual conduct, then those who do not regard those behaviors as normal lose all credibility. For instance, if someone is stricken with, say, cancer, dementia, arthritis, multiple sclerosis, influenza, meningitis, or some other physical disorder, no reasonable individual will hold that person accountable for developing it. Perhaps their behaviors may have prompted or facilitated the sickness to emerge, but essentially it is biologically or organically based. It was brought on through heredity, the process of aging, or some other natural cause. On the other hand, if someone has a disorder brought on by poor thinking processes, traumatic formative years, distorted interpretations of events, seeking an escape from reality, or some other related difficulty, it is caused by the individual's response to the surrounding environment or their nurturing. It is not genetic, the person did not inherit the difficulty; rather, it emerged from an inorganic cause. No matter what dysfunction the individual experienced, they chose their sexual expression as a response to their perceptions and interpretations regarding certain influential life events. For the record, there is no unchallenged credible evidence let alone proof to the contrary.

---

[55] https://statesmanjournal.com/story/news/2017/12/28.

A sympathetic press and predominantly secular mindset prompt society to treat those who disagree as unscientific and obsolete. Anyone who dares to question the normality of transgender identity, transsexual identity, homosexuality, gender fluidity, or a host of other related phenomena as not being a natural, organically based condition is ostracized, their businesses boycotted or sued, and their ideas regarded as ignorant at best. They are told that they need to be educated and enlightened to accept the normalcy of homosexuality, transgender identity, transsexual identity, non-binary sexual expression as well as gender non-conformity.[56]

Nevertheless, numerous studies that deal with several aspects of the transgender phenomenon arrive at conclusions at odds with what the mainstream cultural warriors who promote that behavior would have society believe. The vast majority of these inquiries, in their attempt to locate organic causation, investigate the biological perspective of the matter by examining brain structure, size, and shape among a host of other criteria.[57] Dick Ferdinand (D. F.) Swaab, the noted Dutch neurobiologist, has researched and published extensively on this topic. He noted a number

---

[56] https://liveabout.com/how-to-defeat-homophobic-arguments-1414925, May 23, 2019; accessed July 17, 2019. https://transequality.org/issues/resources/supporting-the-transgender-people-in-your..., July 9, 2016; accessed July 17, 2019.

[57] See, for example, Shawna Williams, "Are the Brains of Transgender People Different from Those of Cisgender People?" *The Scientist*, March 12, 2018 (accessed July 17, 2019); Boston University Medical Center, "Transgender: Evidence on the biological nature of gender identity," *Science Daily*, www.sciencedaily.com/releases/2015/02/150213112317.htm (accessed July 17, 2019); Joshua D. Safer. Evidence Supporting the Biologic Nature of Gender Identity. *Endocrine Practice* February, 2015. DOI: 10.4158/EP14351.RA. Daniel Trotta, "Born this way? Researchers explore the science of gender identity," *Science News* August 3, 2017; and Ricki Lewis, "Here's what

of differences in the brains of transgenders and cisgenders.[58] However, his research is primarily completed postmortem. The subjects, transgender brains, are compared with those of deceased cisgenders. Researchers then tend to find various miniscule differences and conclude that it is a biological issue causing some to be transgender. However, many of these studies find contradictory evidence.[86] Thus, a major problem emerges in that the scientists are not making an accurate comparison. They operate under the unproven and undocumented presupposition that the cause and effect relationship initiates in the brain and results with the behavior. What is located in the brain must be the controlling factor in the behavior, thus relegating sexual non-conformity into the biological realm and removing the psychological, psychiatric, emotional, or environmental component. However, little has been done to examine the phenomenon in reverse. Perhaps the behavior alters the brain. There is no debate that the brain changes throughout a person's life. Extensive research demonstrates conclusively that through brain plasticity some areas of that organ become more active while others less so. Certain regions expand while others diminish. Many of these changes are precipitated by thought

we really know about transgender genetics—so far," *Genetic Literacy Project*, March 29, 2018 (accessed July 17, 2019).

[58] Cisgender refers to people whose sexual identity is congruent with their birth sex.

[86] "Transsexualism: A Different Viewpoint to Brain Changes," Mohammed-Reza Mohammadi and Ali Khalegi, *Clinical Psychopharmacology and Neuroscience 2018, 16(2):136-143 (accessed July 17, 2019)*

patterns, thinking processes, concepts, behavior, and cultural exposure, among other activities and experiences.[59]

Furthermore, Sven Mueller of Ghent University noted "that it remains unclear how those differences developed."[60] Because of adult brain plasticity, any noted difference may or may not have been present at birth. The evidence that Swaab collected, although impressive, is quite possibly, if not probably, being misinterpreted, resulting in erroneous conclusions. Nevertheless, many of those searching for a biological cause jump on his research and conclusions to argue that it proves their case. But actually Swaab's studies provide the same amount of evidence that supports an inorganic or non-biological causality for the behavior. Moreover, in his presentation titled "A Review of Gender Dysphoria," Hamidreza Toufighi with the Tehran University of Medical Sciences declared that "masculinity, femininity, and gender identity may result more from postnatal life events than from prenatal hormonal organization." He related that "genetic causes of gender dysphoria are under study but no candidate genes have been identified." Although comparative "[brain] imaging studies have shown changes in white matter tracts, cerebral blood flow, and cerebral activation patterns in patients with gender dysphoria," those research "studies have not been replicated." He continued to explain that "for a number of sexually dimorphic brain structures or processes, signs of masculinization or feminization are observable in transsexual individuals, which during hormonal treatment, partly seem to further adjust to

---

59   Debbie Hampton, "Neuroplasticity: The 10 Fundamentals of Rewiring Your Brain," https://reset.me/ October 28, 2015, (accessed July 17, 2019).

60   Shawna Williams "Brains of Transgender People".

characteristics of the desired sex." Nevertheless, in conclusion, "it appears that the data are quite inhomogeneous, mostly not replicated, and in many cases available only for male transsexuals transitioning to female."[61] Thus, it becomes essentially yet another scientific study denying the existence of a "transsexual or transgender gene."

Another criticism of the solely organic approach is the extensive incorporation of non-biological terminology in the definition of gender dysphoria as espoused by the 2013 DSM-V. Mohammed-Reza Mohammadi notes that "transsexualism refers to a condition or belief which results in gender dysphoria in individuals and makes them insist that their biological gender is different from their psychological and experienced gender."[62] The DSM-V, in describing the condition, utilizes terminology such as "a marked incongruence between one's experienced gender and one's primary and/or secondary sex characteristics." The next four traits begin with the words "a strong desire," while the final one reads "a strong conviction that one has the typical feelings and reactions of the other gender."[63]

Note the three words: experienced, desire, and conviction. None of these are clearly biological terms. Rather, they reflect a psychological, emotional, or psychiatric tendency. "Transgender children often affirm

---

[61] Hamidriza Toufighi, "A Review of Gender Dysphoria," Presentation given at the Tehran University of Medical Sciences, December 2017.

[62] Mohammed-Reza Mohammadi, "A Different Look," 136.

[63] Hamidriza Toufighi, "A Review of Gender Dysphoria."; Kenneth J. Zucker, "Chapter 4: The DSM-5 Diagnostic Criteria for Gender Dysphoria," in Carlo Trombetta, Giovanni Liguori, Michele Bertolotta, eds. Management of Gender Dysphoria: A Multidisciplinary Approach," (New York: Springer-Verlag, 2015). DOI: 10.1007/978-88-470-5696-1

an internal gender identity opposite from their assigned gender; however, there can be fluidity in the spectrum of maleness and femaleness. Gender dysphoria refers to the distress from the discordance between one's affirmed, or desired, gender and the gender assigned at birth." Later the authors indicate that "a significant proportion of transgender youth struggle with mental health issues and all guidelines require close communication with mental health providers. Children with gender dysphoria have a higher risk of behavioral and emotional issues as well as a higher risk of suicidal ideation and attempts."[64] Essentially, gender dysphoria is described as the difference between one's biological sex and the sex that an individual feels like or more closely identifies with psychologically. It is, thus, more of an emotional issue than a biological matter. This becomes particularly evident when it is combined with the fact that transgenders tend to struggle with mental health issues at rates higher than the general public. When referring to gender dysphoria, highly acclaimed plastic surgeon and editor in chief of *Reconstruction Surgery and Anaplastology*, Carlo Melloni, noted that it "is no longer considered a mental disorder of the sexual sphere but is perceived as a strong incongruence [between the gender an individual identifies with] and their biological sex.... This inconsistency creates an illness such that the individual experiences a clinically significant distress."[65]

The operative concept that one can clearly identify in all these

---

[64] Spack NP, Roberts SA (2015) Caring for Transgender Youth. *J Yoga Phys Ther* 5: 213. doi:10.4172/2157-7595.1000213.

[65] Carlo Melloni, "Management of Gender Dysphoria and Creation of a Gender Team," *Reconstructive Surgery and Anaplastology* Vol. 5, Issue 2, 2016, 5:117 p. 1, Palermo, Italy.

definitions is the emotion of feeling. The phenomenon is essentially psychological, psychiatric, or non-organic rather than biological or organic. If someone experiences physical pain, there is typically a biological or natural cause. The condition is organic and normally traced to something tangible within the body. Yet in the definitions provided by mental health providers themselves, along with those who experience gender dysphoria, the basic biological or organic component is absent. This does not in any way state, imply, or infer that the person's feeling is not real, imagined, or psychosomatic. Rather it is not organic but inorganic. Hence, its source is removed from the biological etiology and brought into the realm of psychological, psychiatric, intellectual, sociological, attitudinal, emotional, or other environmental, non-organic cause. All of this brings one to the point that a person is not "born this way," but rather "becomes this way" through a set of perceptions brought on by a series of events, an understanding of life experiences, thought processes, or even thinking patterns. Perhaps the decision to be transgender was unconscious or made while the individual did not demonstrate control over his or her intellectual or emotional faculties. Nevertheless, a decision was made. Yet if one still refuses to accept that a selection occurred, there clearly was a deliberate, willful, and cognitive choice made to act upon that thought.

"Human Sexuality is an objective biological trait: 'XY' and 'XX' are genetic markers of health, not genetic markers of some disorder," said Michelle Cretella of the American College of Pediatrics. "No one is born with a gender," rather everyone has "a biological sex." Gender is a construct of sociology and psychology, not biology. "An individual's belief," feeling, sensation, or identification as something that they are not "is at best a sign of confused thinking." The standing authority on such matters, the DSM-V reports that "as many as 98% of gender-confused boys and 88% of gender-confused girls eventually accept their biological sex after naturally passing through puberty." Finally, she noted that suicide rates are "20 times greater among adults who use cross-sex hormones and undergo sex reassignment surgery, even in Sweden which is among the most LGBTQ affirming nations."[66]

An academic study published in 2014 analyzed individuals with gender dysphoria approved for sex reassignment (also referred to gender confirmation or gender affirmation surgery) plagued with personality disorders. Interestingly, the majority was diagnosed with at least one of over a dozen inorganic maladies. For instance, well over half, 57.1%, carried the label of narcissism. Nearly 40% were obsessive-compulsive, over a third masochistic-sadistic, while a quarter dealt with paranoia. Those with mood or psychotic disorders were excluded from the study, a move which probably diminished the frequency of syndromes. Yet the average number of personality disorders suffered by those in this research was three in addition to gender dysphoria. Thus prompting the astute individual to ponder, if those experiencing gender dysphoria have so many inorganic or non-biological personality disorders, what is the possibility that the dysphoria also falls into that category?[67]

Another aspect of gender dysphoria that receives too little balanced

---

[66] Michella Cretella, MD, President of ACP; Paul McHugh, MD University Distinguished Service Professor of Psychiatry at Johns Hopkins Medical School; Quentin Van Meter, MD, VP, ACP, Pediatric Endocrinologist, "Gender Ideology Harms Children," Position Statement of the American College of Pediatricians, March 21, 2016, Updated September, 2017.

[67] Mazaheri Meybodi A, Hajebi A, Ghanbari Jolfaei A. "The Frequency of Personality

attention is the mental health of those who transition from one bio-logical sex to another. Rather than the panacea as mainstream media frequently portray to the general public, there are many with serious regrets. For example, a 2014 follow-up reflecting on male-to-female indi-viduals reported some surprising results. This study was completed by sending questionnaires to 254 male-to-female transsexuals. Fewer than half (46.9%) of the patients filled out and returned the feedback request. The mean was 5.05 years after surgery. A vast majority, 90.2%, said their expectations for life as a woman were fulfilled postoperatively. However, those expectations were never delineated. If one does not expect much, then that person probably will not be too surprised when it does not occur. They claim that 85.4% saw themselves as women. But that means nearly 15% did not. Furthermore, only two-thirds (67%) were satisfied with their life as it is now, which at the very least implies that one-third remained unsatisfied.[68] If transgender identity was biological rather than inorganic, one could reliably presume that surgical intervention would produce a higher rate of success. The authors advised to interpret the rates of satisfaction with caution, because less than half even bothered to return the canvass. Yet if this surgery resolved or at least minimized the distress precipitated by these 254 patients facing gender dysphoria, one would surely surmise that their satisfaction with the results and the questionnaire-return rate would be significantly higher. Moreover, this

Disorders in Patients with Gender Identity Disorder," Med J Islam Repub Iran, September 10, 2014, Vol. 28:90.

[68] "Satisfaction with Male-to-Female Gender Reassignment Surgery: Results of a Retrospective Analysis," (Hess J., Rossi Neto R., Panic L., Rubben H., Senf W., Dtsch Arztebl Int.), 2014; 111(0047):795-801.

study only incorporates male-to-female transsexuals. The scientific community is blatantly remiss by their minimal research on female-to-male transsexuals.

Another scholarly approach may be located at the "What We Know Project," an online research portal based at the Center for the Study of Inequality at Cornell University. It expends significant effort studying and analyzing the social, economic, political status, and condition of non-binary sexually expressing people. Dr. Nathaniel Frank, the project director, is, among other things, a political activist promoting gay, lesbian, and transsexual rights. He and his husband reside in Brooklyn. Moreover, it is essential to note that the man in charge has an agenda sympathetic with the LGBTQ policy advocates.[69] Recently, the center examined the question, "What does the scholarly research say about the effect of gender transition on transgender well-being?" They "conducted a systematic literature review of all peer-reviewed articles published in English between 1991 and June 2017 that assess the effect of gender transition on transgender well-being."[70] Their highly skewed analysis "determined that 93% of the 52 studies found that gender transition improves the overall

---

[69] See, for instance, the "What We Know Project" website. https://whatweknow. inequality.cornell.edu/about/about-dr-nathaniel-frank/.

[70] A few scholarly publications cited in the "What We Know" research include the *Journal of Sexual Medicine, International Journal of Transgenderism, Journal of Gay and Lesbian Mental Health, Journal of Sex and Marital Therapy, International Journal of Sexual Health, Psychology of Sexual Orientation and Gender Diversity, Sexual and Relationship Therapy, Journal of Psychology and Human Sexuality* as well as the *Archives of Sexual Behavior*. Such titles prompt suspicions regarding objectivity and academic honesty to say the very least.

well-being of transgender people, while 4 (7%) report mixed or null findings." Included in this glowing report of transsexual transition was the Hess research previously cited. It certainly was not congruent with the Cornell interpretation. Specifically, they concluded "that gender transition is highly effective in treating gender dysphoria and can improve their well-being." Disappointingly, there is no apparent definition of the nebulous terms "highly effective" and "well-being." Among other conclusions, Frank and his colleagues also claim that "regrets following gender transition are extremely rare, from .3–3.8%."[71]

Incongruence between the Hess and Frank research results is worthy of further examination. These significant discrepancies in a single study prompt the question: If Cornell's project reported such misleading conclusions and interpretations, how accurate and trustworthy can its findings actually be?[72] Moreover, there is no distinction regarding those who transitioned—were they female to male or vice versa? Furthermore, as previously noted, the Hess study was based on fewer than half of the patients selected for the research, but no record is supplied regarding the questionnaire rate return of any studies used by Cornell. Therefore, the results of Frank's research are tenuous at best. Also, there is no way to determine the honesty of those who completed and returned their survey. If a person spent tens of thousands of dollars on a procedure with

---

[71] https://whatweknow.inequality.cornell.edu "What Does the Scholarly Research say about the Effect of Gender Transition on Transgender Well-Being?" What We Know Project, Cornell University, 2017. Accessed July 17, 2019.

[72] The discrepancies being the variance between the studies regarding the numbers of extraordinarily high degree of well-being of postoperative trans patients and the exceptionally low number of regrets, not to mention the paltry participation rate.

which they are not happy, how likely are they to admit their remorse to researchers? As a final note, quantitative studies based on questionnaires are popular because they tend to be far less expensive than other techniques. Hence, the results are frequently not as reliable or perhaps even as valid as other more costly and lengthy methodologies. Any analysis must be couched in the most cautious terms, a procedure not utilized by the Cornell project.

In 2018, Hess and several others published a study titled "Sexuality after Male to Female Gender Affirmation Surgery." This project was based on a survey sent to the 254 individuals who underwent the medical procedure at the "Department of Urology, University Hospital Essen, Germany, between 2004 and 2010. All patients were contacted by mail using their last known address and asked if they would be willing to answer the questionnaire. In cases of invalid addresses, the local residents' registration offices were contacted in order to reconsign a new questionnaire." Unfortunately, this study was quite limited like most and far too nebulous to deduce a pattern. Indeed, the return rate was just over 43% (119 of 254 patients). Although the study found that 74% (of the 43%) were satisfied with postoperative sexual intercourse that is a small aspect of gender fulfillment. Furthermore, an ironic component of the project's respondents is that 37.6% claimed to be homosexual, 33.7% heterosexual, 22.8% bisexual, and 5.9% asexual. It indicates that gender affirmation or sex change surgery did not resolve the ostensible gender dysphoria.[73]

---

[73] Hess, J. *et al.* "Sexuality after Male-to-Female Gender Affirmation Surgery." *BioMed Research International* Volume 2018, Article ID 9037979 Available from: https://www. researchgate.net/publication/325400870_Sexuality_after_Male-to-Female_Gender_ Affirmation_Surgery (accessed October 11, 2019).

Other publications with a broader reading audience include Brynn Tannehill's "Myths about Transition Regrets" published in the February 2, 2016, online edition of the *Huffington Post*. The author is a board member of the Trans United Fund, an organization to promote and expand the socioeconomic-political power and influence of transgenders, a post that at the very least taints her impartiality. Jack Drescher's "Five Myths on Being Transgender" was published in the *Washington Post* on May 13, 2016. He is a member of the Association of LGBTQ (formerly Gay and Lesbian) Psychiatrists, authored numerous books and articles on the subject, but perhaps most importantly is an ardent activist for the homosexual and transsexual political agenda. Hence, his objectivity is at best thinly veiled.

Having established a sense of those who support transsexual transition and trivialize the notion that a significant number regret the change, a different approach is due for those who are seriously damaged by it and may even want to reverse the procedure. Stella Morabito wrote on November 11, 2014, "Trouble in Transtopia: Murmurs of Sex Change Regret." Her article in the *Federalist* claimed that the "transgender lobby actively polices and suppresses discussion of sex change regret, and claims it's rare (no more than '5%')." She continued, "However, if you do decide to 'detransition' to once again identify with the sex in your DNA, talking about it will get you targeted by trans activists. So, it's a challenge to understand the scope of regret for sex change surgery." Her bold statement is just that, but with what evidence can she support it? She related the account of Alan Finch, who confessed in a 2004 interview with *The Guardian* that "transsexualism was invented by psychiatrists....." He continued by admitting that his gender affirmation (or sex change) surgery has "all been a terrible misadventure. I've never been a woman, just Alan...[74]

In her monograph *Gender Hurts: A Feminist Analysis of the Politics of Transgenderism*, Sheila Jeffreys cited the account of Heath Russell, a lesbian who mentioned the possibility of her transgender identity to a therapist who simply accepted it and prescribed hormonal treatment. Those in the trans community warned her to avoid any therapist who may question her alleged condition. Ironically, she had misgivings about the transition process herself, but her trans associates told her to stay the course. After experiencing some health difficulties and learning of others, she very publicly ended her transition, announcing it in a television interview. The trans community, however, did not take kindly to her action and males responded with unspeakable insults, death threats, and other intimidating actions. Females, on the other hand, told her to take responsibility for her behavior and keep quiet because her vocal objections were "undermining the medical understanding of transgenderism."[75]

Walter Heyer was born male, transitioned to a female, and lived as one for several years before he realized his error and "returned" to his birth sex. The subsequent anger and open hostility he experienced from his acquaintances and associates were overwhelming and threatening. Thus, it becomes highly apparent that detransitioning to one's original sex may be met with extreme emotional and physical danger. Hence, one who might not be strong-willed or unable to handle successfully such intense criticism and ostracism could very well remain unfilled in their

---

[74] David Batty, "Sex Changes are not Effective," *The Guardian*, July 30, 2004.

[75] Selwyn Duke, "The Transgender Con?"

transitioned condition. Ophthalmologist Rene Richards, in a 2007 interview with Joyce Wadler, revealed herself as an ambiguous individual who did not admit that she regretted her sex change operation. Contrariwise, she has experienced remorse for many of its consequences. Indeed, the interview was titled "The Lady Regrets." Wadler commented, "And as she wearies of the interview, her body language seems to become more traditionally male, suggesting an athlete who is wearying of the game." Various other interviews demonstrate that she is highly complicated, filled with conundrums regarding her earlier surgery.[76]

A fourth individual, Mike Penner, a sportswriter for the *Los Angeles Times*, has a heart-wrenching story. Throughout much of his life, he demonstrated signs of gender dysphoria. As a boy while at home alone, he sometimes dressed in his mother's attire and makeup. Yet overcome by guilt and remorse removed all before anyone saw him. Later he became heavily involved in sports, especially soccer and in 1983 began his journalistic career with the *LA Times*. Three years later, he married Lisa Dillman, also a sportswriter. But his deep yearning to be female continued unabated. When his wife learned of Penner's gender dysphoria is perhaps known only to her, but it occurred sometime within the next two decades. On April 26, 2007, he wrote, "Transsexualism is a complicated and widely misunderstood medical condition. It is a natural occurrence—unusual, no question, but natural." He erroneously contended that "recent studies have shown that such physiological factors as genetics and hormonal fluctuations during pregnancy can significantly affect how our brains are 'wired' at birth." Thus, he determined that "as extensive therapy and testing have confirmed, my brain was wired female."

---

[76] Joyce Wadler, "The Lady Regrets," *New York Times,* February 2, 2007.

He concluded that "when you reach the point when one gender causes heartache and unbearable discomfort, and the other brings more joy and fulfillment than you ever imagined possible, it shouldn't take two tons of bricks to fall in order to know what to do." He soon departed for a lengthy vacation and returned as Christine Daniels, the name under which they wrote for about a year. They then took a second extended leave of absence and returned as Mike Penner. Shortly thereafter, tragedy struck as he ended his life. A private funeral was held in his memory to eliminate any press coverage. However, the LGBTQ community in Los Angeles held a memorial highly publicized by the gay press.[77]

Many others made the choice to transition from their birth sex to another. Billy Burleigh, for example, was abused sexually as a child and in time developed gender dysphoria. According to the documentary "I Want My Sex Back," he wanted to be like his sisters and in time began taking hormones and underwent gender affirmation surgery. Initially, he hoped that his life would improve. However, after seven years of living as a woman, he realized that his sexually related problems would not end, so he opted to have surgery to transition back to a man. After he adjusted to living as a male, he examined some pictures taken during his time as a woman. They reflected a disappointed man who realized that those years were wasted, so he destroyed the photos. Burleigh has since married and lives with his wife in an undisclosed location.[78]

Another example is Rene Jax, who was born male but experienced

---

[77] Steve Friess, "Mike Penner, Christian Daniels: A Tragic Love Story," *Los Angeles Weekly*, August 19, 2010.

[78] Mikhail Berynin, Director, "I Want My Sex Back," (Russian Television Documentary, 2018).

a challenging childhood that included an alcoholic and absentee father, among other things. Gender dysphoria emerged and beginning at the age of 20 he began living as a female. She was treated with hormones and underwent sex reassignment surgery. Yet her gender dysphoria did not dissipate. She and several doctors concluded that the real problem was that she did not like herself. Nothing she or anyone else did could relieve her symptoms. Until she grew to accept and like herself, she would never be happy or content. When Rene got to that point, she opted not to return to her birth sex because she could not see the point. She realized that if she detransitioned back to a man, her position as a social pariah would remain. Therefore, she speaks to those who may be considering gender reassignment surgery and tells them that it will not resolve any gender dysphoria issues they may be experiencing. It is far better to learn to like and accept oneself. No change in sex will solve their difficulties.[79]

In an interesting twist on sex change regret, *The Telegraph* of London published an interview with professor Miroslav Djordjevic who expressed concern about the lack of research on transgender people changing their minds and undergoing reversal surgery. Djordjevic, an acclaimed surgeon and researcher who performs about 100 sex change surgeries annually, divides his time between New York's Mount Sinai Hospital and his clinic in Belgrade, Serbia. Djordjevic told psychotherapist James Caspian that he was first contacted by a patient wanting a reversal about five years ago. The number of reversals has continued to grow. Currently, he has two patients completing the return to their birth sex and another six prospective surgeries. According to Djordjevic, some patients report crippling depression and suicidal ideation after their reassignment operation. The

---

[79] Mikhail Berynin, "I Want My Sex Back."

conversation prompted Caspian to research the trend of sex change surgery regret for a master's degree. But after preliminary research, Bath Spa University rejected his proposal. Officials told him they were afraid of online criticism especially from the powerful transgender lobby about a "politically incorrect" topic. A baffled Djordjevic attested, "Definitely, reversal surgery and regret in transgender persons is one of the very hot topics. Generally, we have to support all research in this field."[80]

Furthermore, Djordjevic is deeply concerned about the growing pressure to treat patients at younger ages. In the last twenty years, the average age of his patients has dropped from 45 to 21. He refuses to perform the procedure on anyone younger than 18, but fears the World Professional Association for Transgender Health will soon reduce their guidelines for gender reassignment surgeries to include minors. Interestingly, the rates of minors seeking treatment for gender dysphoria continue to elevate. In April 2017, for instance, the only clinic in England that assessed "minors for gender identity development services reported that it saw 2,016 referrals in the previous 12 months, a 42% increase from the year before, on top of a 104% increase from the year before that." Furthermore, "the number of children being treated for gender identity disorder at Scotland's Sandyford Clinic in Glasgow quadrupled in the past three

---

[80] Caspian accused the university of suppressing important research and raised more than 23,000 pounds to challenge the ruling. Moreover, since 2017 he said that 50 people contacted him expressing regret about their transition to the opposite sex and wanted to reverse the procedure. Nevertheless, on February 19, 2019, a judge refused permission for Caspian to continue with his bid for judicial review. Not surprisingly, Caspian said he thought the decision was wrong and that he would look into appealing it. https://www.somersetlive.co.uk/news.somersetnews/bath-spa-university-James-caspian-2557060 accessed November 3, 2019.

years, according to an article published this week in the Glasgow newspaper *The Herald*, from under 50 in 2013 to more than 200 cases last year."[81] Hence, it is clearly apparent that an increasing number appear to hope that sex reassignment surgery will prove beneficial. An assertion that many claim will merely exacerbate the challenge of gender dysphoria. The few accounts mentioned here represent real people, not statistical data.[82] Countless others have similar stories, all are painful, pitiful, and pathetic. One can hardly read them and not generate even a modicum of sadness. Yet there are literally thousands of victims in that position.

In 2014, the American Society for Suicide Prevention and the Williams Institute, an LGBTQ-focused research organization associated with the UCLA School of Law, released a study alleging that over 40% of transgenders had attempted suicide at least once. The rate among the general public is roughly one-tenth of that amount, 4.6%. Thus, most press and media outlets quickly offered their theories. They tended to claim that the statistic provided solid undeniable evidence regarding the extent of bullying and discrimination faced by the transgender, transsexual, persons with gender dysphoria, and other LGBTQ segments of the population. Suicidal ideation offered the only escape from their personal distress. However, their trigger-happy response was, to say the least, short-sighted, misleading, and even inaccurate.[83]

---

[81] Kiley Crossland, "One renowned surgeon says more study is needed of why some people 'detransition,'" *World Digital*, October 6, 2017. Accessed November 3, 2019.

[82] For another example, one with a happier ending, see Anne Reed, "From transgendered to transformed," *American Family Association Journal*, December, 2018.

[83] Brynn Tannehill, "The Truth About Transgender Suicide," *Huffington Post*, November

Indeed, a cursory examination of the report reveals a vastly different interpretation. In the methods and limitations segment of the study, its authors reveal no fewer than five concessions that potentially if not conclusively invalidate any results. The research began in the fall of "2008 and was distributed online and on paper through over 900 organizations that were known venues for contact with the transgender community throughout the United States." The research sample included "6,456 self-identified transgender and gender non-conforming adults aged 18 and over." There was no hint of scientific sampling, merely those who responded to an inquiry. Secondly, they state that the survey consisted of one question, "Have you ever attempted suicide?" with a simple binary response, yes or no, notwithstanding the fact that researchers are aware "that using this question alone in surveys can inflate the percentage of affirmative responses." Some "respondents may use it to communicate self-harm behavior that is not a 'suicide attempt,' such as seriously contemplating suicide, planning for suicide, or engaging in self-harm behavior without the intent to die." A third problematic issue is that the survey "did not directly explore mental health status and history, which have been identified as important risk factors for both attempted and completed suicide in the general population." Fourthly, "since the NTDS utilized convenience sampling, it is unclear how representative the respondents are of the overall US transgender/gender non-conforming adult population. Further, the survey's focus on discrimination may have resulted in wider participation by persons who had suffered negative life experiences due to antitransgender bias."

14, 2015; Laura Ungar, "Transgender people face alarmingly high rate of suicide," *USA Today,* August 16, 2015.

Another difficulty is that this survey "captured information about suicide attempts, not completed suicide." There is, however, no question that males are significantly more likely to succeed in this action although women attempt it more frequently. The study, thus, is highly flawed and in no uncertain terms fails to provide sufficient answers in response to the hype generated by mainstream media. Nevertheless, the study did show some ironic twists which never made it into the news. Perhaps most notable is that "those respondents who said they had received transition-related health care or wanted to have it someday were more likely to report having attempted suicide than those who said they did not want it." This despite the fact that transgenders are often told that the best therapy for their situation is gender affirmation surgery. "This pattern was observed across all transition-related services and procedures that were explored in the NTDS."[84]

If transgender identity was biological, it appears highly unusual as well as unlikely that an excessively high percentage would take such drastic action. Evidence clearly indicates an inorganic causation. Therefore, it appears that contrary to what the transsexual/transgender/gender fluid community would have the public believe, they utilize misleading studies, biased data, and unreliable sources with minimal validity to promote

---

[84] Ann Haas, Philip L. Rodgers, Jody Herman. *Suicide Attempts Among Transgender and Gender Non-conforming Adults Findings of the National Transgender Discrimination Survey.* American Foundation for Suicide Prevention/The Williams Institute UCLA College of Law. January, 2014. For further analysis, see the website https://williamsinstitute.law.ucla.edu; 4thWaveNow.com, "The 41% trans suicide rate: a tale of flawed data and lazy journalists"; Daniel Payne, "The Transgender Suicide Rate Isn't Due to Discrimination," *The Federalist,* July 7, 2016.

their agenda. They tend to hide behind the scientific community even if the information it provides is highly inaccurate and often intentionally misleading, or the highly tainted product of individuals with social, cultural, economic, and political intentions. Furthermore, they work diligently to silence any who detransition or leave their God-dishonoring lifestyle. Thus, one may logically conclude that the transsexual argument regarding the organic causes of their condition is not without considerable disagreement. Many scientists researching this topic have ulterior motives and are merely looking for genes or other organic components that could cause any non-binary sexual condition. There will undoubtedly be more allegedly scientific studies and discoveries regarding the etiology of non-binary sexual expression. There will be additional tear-jerking stories of people detransitioning, and the LGBTQ community will continue to influence both the American Psychological Association and the American Psychiatric Association. But the fact remains that there is "no gay gene," nor is there any transgender or transsexual gene, and no matter what certain researchers and their popularized studies may contend, gender dysphoria and its subsequent consequences are prompted primarily by inorganic causes.

CHAPTER 5

DOES ACCEPTANCE TRULY BRING RELIEF?

"Thus says the LORD, 'Cursed is the man who trusts in mankind and makes flesh his strength, and whose heart turns away from the LORD. For he will be like a bush in the desert and will not see when prosperity comes, but will live in stony wastes in the wilderness, a land of salt without inhabitant. Blessed is the man who trusts in the LORD and whose trust is the LORD. For he will be like a tree planted by the water, that extends its roots by a stream and will not fear when the heat comes; but its leaves will be green, and it will not be anxious in a year of drought nor cease to yield fruit'"

JEREMIAH 17:5–8

Various spiritually oriented adages permeate twenty-first-century American society. Such expressions may sound great and on the surface appear to hold considerable merit. Thus many latch on to them and cling tenaciously. Some examples include "God helps those who help themselves," "God will never give you more than you can handle," "This too shall pass," and "When God closes a door, He opens a window."[85] Although frequently stated, even by evangelicals, they do not reflect biblical teaching. Satan often couches worldly concepts in religious jargon. Thus it is essential that believers have a solid understanding of Scripture. Moreover, "Be diligent to present yourself approved to God as a workman who does not need to be ashamed, accurately handling the word of truth."[86]

This prompts yet another popular notion that deals with widely accepted spiritual and conventional wisdom. It reads something like this: "If someone experiences any type of setback and cannot seem to work through it they need to accept whatever has occurred. By doing so they will finally be able to stop struggling emotionally and achieve the peace, courage, and strength to move forward." The statement also infers the reverse notion that a lack of acceptance guarantees continued disappointment, discouragement, and perhaps depression. Hence, acceptance is in many ways viewed as a physical, mental, intellectual, emotional and perhaps spiritual panacea. It will provide relief when nothing else seems to do so. However, a closer examination of this concept and its application suggests that what society and many well-meaning Christians approve as sage advice should itself be more carefully scrutinized and analyzed.

---

[85] Laura Polk, "Seven Christian sayings that aren't Christian at all," *Crosswalk*, April 22, 2016, accessed February 12, 2019.

[86] 2 Timothy 2:15

A believer faced with familial or relational transgender identity, transsexual identity, nonbinary sexual expression, or gender nonconformity often experiences emotions similar to those that accompany any significant but disappointing change or event in a person's life. It could include examples such as an accident, forced termination of employment, financial setback, emotional crisis, separation/divorce, or any type of major deprivation. They may, for instance, feel like they have lost a friend, a family member, or a close associate, often triggering the emotion of grief. Not that the individual is physically dead, but that the person with whom they associated no longer exists, hence the sense of deep personal loss.

Two widely accepted examples illustrate the popular notion of acceptance. Those who seek counseling regarding their situation often learn that they are experiencing intense sorrow. A therapist may relay that grief has five universal but nonconsecutive stages. That is, one may experience the initial phase and move to the next two but then return to the first or second before arriving at the fourth. With the first anniversary of the grief-prompting event, the individual often returns to the depths of initial grief. The five stages include denial, anger, bargaining, depression, and acceptance. These are, however, based solely upon the late Elisabeth Kübler-Ross's highly misleading albeit popularly accepted manuscript *On Death and Dying*. The Swiss-American psychiatrist's salient work resulted from a single non-replicated study of a number of patients who confronted fatal illnesses and how they came to terms with their diagnoses. After compiling and analyzing the feelings expressed by these patients, Kübler-Ross determined that these five emotions were universal among the subjects she studied. When the people accepted their condition, negative emotional responses ceased and they sensed contentment. Not that her conclusions are without merit, but the fact remains that she focused only on a single circumstance, those who encountered terminal illness. Furthermore she neglected to examine those who faced the death of a loved one or a personal loss not leading to their own demise, such as the loss of a job, a financial crisis, or any other disappointing, life-changing event. Additionally, perhaps by deliberate choice or honest oversight, the thanatologist omitted addressing the impending death of those individuals, contrary to her book's title. Rather, it was patients coming to terms with their dire prognoses. Thus, when applying the results of her investigation, one must be highly selective because her research was as well. But often a pioneering study receives excessive attention and is accepted with considerably less scrutiny than do subsequent research projects on similar topics. Thus her study was almost universally accepted and applied to far more situations than was appropriate.

A much more balanced and perceptive approach to acceptance may be secured in Ruth Davis Konigsberg's *The Truth About Grief*.[87] It provides room for considerably more latitude among those who grieve, particularly those for whom this manuscript addresses, believers who face gender non-conformity within their close familial, relational, or occupational circles. Davis Konigsberg contended that "probably the most accurate predictors of how someone will grieve are their personality and temperament before the loss." She also noted: "The truth is that there is no agreed-upon list of emotions that one has to experience, that there's little evidence to support

---

[87] One must be careful about any human work that claims to have the truth; that is reserved for Scripture alone. Ruth Davis Konigsberg, *The Truth About Grief: The Myth of Its Five Stages and the New Science of Loss* (Simon and Schuster, 2011).

the notion that one has to do 'grief work' in order to heal...."[88] Although society tends to prefer a one-size-fits-all method of dealing with grief such as the five stages, life cannot objectively or correctly be explained in a simplistic formula. Therefore Davis Konigsberg's work is of significantly greater benefit to those experiencing a major deprivation. When dealing with issues regarding sexual dysphoria, it is essential to keep in mind that everyone—the gender nonconformist as well as their families, friends, associates, and others—often experience a variety of emotions, including grief and loss. Nevertheless, through Kübler-Ross's influence, both parties are often egged on toward the same destination: acceptance. Untold counselors, therapists, pastors, well-meaning friends, and well-intentioned associates have for years worked with clients, acquaintances, adherents, and others toward accepting certain situations as immutable. When one arrives at that point in their own psyche, they will begin to experience peace and contentment. However, is this really the desired conclusion?

A second widely dispersed example, the Serenity Prayer, especially the abbreviated version, infers the same concept. It reads, "God, grant me the serenity to accept the things I cannot change, courage to change the things I can, and wisdom to know the difference." On the surface this appears to be sound advice, but a cursory analysis provides an alternate if not more accurate perspective. A problem with Ronald Niebuhr's "prayer" is that although it may contain a kernel of insight, it is loaded

---

[88]   Vanna Lee, "The Exchange: Ruth Davis Konigsberg on Grieving," *The New Yorker*, January 24, 2011, www.newyorker.com, accessed December 5, 2019. For further insight and analysis, see Paul K. Maciejewski *et al.* "An Empirical Examination of the Stage Theory of Grief," *New England Journal of Medicine*, February 21, 2007.

with untruth and certainly does not reflect biblical admonition. A fatalistic mind-set of accepting the things I cannot change is not found in
God's Word. For example, while imprisoned, the apostle Paul wrote to
the Philippian church: "I can do all things through Him who strengthens
me." Paul told his readers not only to confess their sinful condition to
the Lord and invite Him into their hearts as personal savior but also to
allow Him to live His life through them. People needed a changed heart,
not one that accepted their current sin-sated condition. The apostle John
quoted the Lord Jesus in his gospel: "I am the vine, you are the branches;
he who abides in Me and I in him, he bears much fruit, for apart from Me
you can do nothing."[89] John related that Christ wants people not only to
accept their sinful condition but also to allow Him to provide salvation
as well as their very being, even to the point of abiding in Him. This is
brought about only by a changed heart. Moreover, acceptance certainly
does not apply to the Lord's actions. He knew that following their creation
Adam, Eve, and subsequently all humanity would deliberately, willfully,
and cognitively choose to sin. The Father could merely have accepted this
event and allowed all humanity to remain eternally separated from Him.
Yet God moved far beyond acceptance and provided the means by which
anyone could opt to accept His sacrifice for sin and enjoy an everlasting relationship with Him. Scripture teaches people not merely to accept
their lost condition, but to move considerably further toward approval
and approbation of the Son's atoning death and resurrection. Indeed, 1
Timothy 1:15 states, "It is a trustworthy statement, deserving full acceptance, that Christ Jesus came into the world to save sinners, among whom
I am foremost of all." Continuing in the same epistle 4:7b–8: "discipline

---

[89] John 15:5

yourself for the purpose of godliness; for bodily discipline is only of little profit, but godliness is profitable for all things, since it holds promise for the present life and also for the life to come." Paul continued in verses 9–10: "It is a trustworthy statement deserving full acceptance. For it is for this we labor and strive, because we have fixed our hope on the living God, who is the Savior of all men, especially of believers."

One might contend that Niebuhr distanced himself from fatalism by asking that God provide the serenity to accept what he could not change, the courage to change the things he could, along with wisdom to know the difference. Nevertheless he essentially requested serenity, courage, and wisdom to accept the immutable. This is not a concept located in the Bible. Indeed, a more effective approach to God is found in James 1:5–6: "But if any of you lacks wisdom, let him ask of God, who gives to all generously and without reproach, and it will be given to him. But he must ask in faith without any doubting, for the one who doubts is like the surf of the sea, driven and tossed by the wind." Examine closely Paul's statement to the Philippians, where he noted: "I can do all things through Him who strengthens me."[90] The apostle acknowledged that in and of himself he was incapable of doing anything, but under the power of the Holy Spirit he could do all things. John related the same thought in a different form in 15:5, when he wrote regarding Jesus that "apart from Me you can do nothing." The fact is that at face value, Niebuhr taught that there are some things I can do; Scripture, though, teaches the opposite. One can do nothing apart from the Lord Jesus. Therefore the question remains, is acceptance truly the optimal end? If one reveals to family, friends, associates, and others that their biological gender construct and mind-set do

---

90   Philippians 4:13

not match, the news can be devastating or highly disconcerting, particularly for those with a high view of Holy Writ. It can most certainly trigger an outpouring of grief among other emotions, as discussed elsewhere. Acceptance is not normally the response of a believer.

A few more biblical admonitions may provide additional insight; take for instance human sinfulness. Jesus Himself teaches that no one is good except God. In fact, even the great King David, a man after God's own heart, wrote in Psalm 14:3: "They have all turned aside, together they have become corrupt; There is no one who does good, not even one." Jeremiah 17:9 reads, "The heart is more deceitful than all else and is desperately sick; who can understand it?" The Holy Spirit convicts people of their own sinfulness, but that is only the first step. Accepting their condition will provide no contentment, calmness, courage, or comfort. Rather, they are not to rest in their new understanding of the human condition, but to agree with God regarding their individual sinfulness and to trust the Lord as personal savior by asking Him to cover their sin with His atoning blood. If acceptance was the destination, all humanity would be doomed to spend eternity separated from their Creator, the crucified One, who rose from the dead. Following salvation, believers move even further by allowing the Holy Spirit to transform them into the image of the Lord Jesus. Indeed, Paul, under the inspiration of the Holy Spirit, penned in Romans 8:29: "For those whom He foreknew, He also predestined to become conformed to the image of His Son…." Evangelicals growing in the Lord will desire to become more Christlike in their conduct, conversation, and character.

Another example may be found in the book of Psalms. Note God's Word in 39:7–8, as David did not merely accept and acknowledge his sin but confessed: "And now, Lord, for what do I wait? My hope is in You. Deliver me from all my transgressions; make me not the reproach of the foolish." Verses 9 and 10 read, "Remove Your plague from me; because of the opposition of Your hand I am perishing. With reproofs You chasten a man for iniquity; You consume as a moth what is precious to him; surely every man is a mere breath." In Psalm 40:1–3, David rejoiced in the Lord's forgiveness: "I waited patiently for the LORD; and He inclined to me and heard my cry. He brought me up out of the pit of destruction, out of the miry clay, and He set my feet upon a rock making my footsteps firm. He put a new song in my mouth, a song of praise to our God; many will see and fear and will trust in the Lord." Had David merely settled for acceptance, the Lord would not have led him to the freedom found in the exalting words in the fortieth psalm. The prophet Isaiah told the godly kings Asa, Uzziah, and Hezekiah not to accept their foolish pride, but to repent when their proud hearts precipitated a less than comforting Word from Jehovah.[91] The book of Jeremiah is replete with the weeping prophet's call toward faithless Judah to pursue Jehovah even as they were taken captive by Nebuchadnezzar's relentless army. When one settles for acceptance they agree with Satan's lie. One may accept that their house was destroyed by fire, but they must also move beyond that point and construct a new one or relocate to a different residence. Another may accept the fact that they are terminally ill, but that certainly should not imply that they are simply to wait for death. God's greatest desire is to have a close, personal, intimate, and growing relationship with His own, and their last days in their earthly body should be spent nourishing the connection with their Savior.

---

91 Further details may be located in 2 Chronicles 16, 26, and 32.

By the same token, the world tells individuals who sense themselves as gender nonconforming that they are to accept it and celebrate it with pride. But this can create a false and temporary sensation that living as their non-biological sex will resolve their sexual or perhaps gender dysphoria. Until one addresses their situation with the Father, through the Son, empowered by the Holy Spirit, nothing below the surface will change. They feel trapped inside a wrongly sexed body and are deceived into thinking that by living as the opposite sex and perhaps undergoing sex reassignment surgery, they will sense completion and fulfillment. If indeed the transition does solve the dysphoria along with the pain and grief, then how does one reconcile the growing numbers who have had the surgery yet in time desire to return to their birth sex?

Humans were created to have fellowship with God and all have a craving for that intimacy. Nothing can fill that void other than the Lord Himself. It is essential that all do come to the point of acceptance from which they may move forward, but the transgender agenda seeks for the wrong type of acceptance. It argues that an individual must accept their sexual dysphoria. Scripture, however, teaches the opposite. In Psalm 139:14, Holy Writ states, "I will give thanks to You, for I am fearfully and wonderfully made; wonderful are Your works, and my soul knows it very well." Jeremiah 1:5 notes, "Before I formed you in the womb I knew you, and before you were born I consecrated you; I have appointed you a prophet to the nations." Psalm 139:13 adds, "For You formed my inward parts; You wove me in my mother's womb." In Isaiah 49:1, the prophet announced, "Listen to Me, O islands, and pay attention, you peoples from afar. The LORD called me from the womb; from the body of my mother He named me." Scripture teaches clearly that the Father knows every person from their mother's womb and that He created them in His image. According to Isaiah 43:1: "But now, thus says the LORD your Creator, O Jacob, and He who formed you, O Israel, 'Do not fear, for I have redeemed you; I have called you by name; you are Mine!'" To argue that one's gender does not match their biological makeup certainly at the very least suggests that God erred in His creation. Sexual or gender transition and perhaps a "sex or gender affirming" operation will not provide the relief they so desperately seek and need.

To become a Christian and experience a relationship with the Father, one must accept and comprehend the words of Christ, who during a conversation with the rich young ruler in Matthew 19:17 declared: "There is only One who is good...." The apostle Paul told the Romans in 3:23: "for all have sinned and fall short of the glory of God." He related in 6:23 of the same epistle, "For the wages of sin is death, but the free gift of God is eternal life in Christ Jesus our Lord." Psalm 53:3 reads, "Every one of them has turned aside; together they have become corrupt; there is no one who does good, not even one." Once one accepts the fact that no one is good, they may move on to confess their sinfulness, helplessness, and hopelessness to God and ask the Father to apply the shed blood of the Lord Jesus upon them. He will place them in an eternal relationship with Him. Their names are written in the Lamb's Book of Life; they are sealed unto the day of redemption and their eternal destiny is secured. Moreover, they are indwelt by the Father, Son, and Holy Spirit. Furthermore, each day as they obey the Lord and live the life of grace, they will become more and more like Him.

The world's perspective, as well as the mind-set of many if not most in the transgender and sexual nonconformist community, contends that humans are good in and of themselves with no need for God or salvation. Their powerful voice has succeeded in frightening many evangelicals into silence. Yet the Word of God has been a foundation of culture for millennia. Many social institutions such as the family, government, and economic systems are rooted deeply in Scripture. It appears highly presumptuous to seek to remove the thousands of years of old rock upon which Western civilization is founded.[92] Indeed, the prophet Isaiah reminded his readers, "So will My Word be which goes forth from My Mouth; it will not return to me empty, without accomplishing what I desire, and without succeeding in the matter for which I sent it."[93]

The transgender, transsexual, and gender nonconformist has, for all practical purposes, drawn the proverbial line in the sand in a futile attempt to silence Scripture. They place their own feelings, ideas, and sensations as the baseline upon which all things are measured. Scripture, in their minds, no longer exists as a barrier to their lifestyle choice. Many seek gender reassignment surgery, hormonal treatment, or other means to transition or perhaps simply to live as they choose. Indeed, one may present as a female or a male depending upon how they may feel.[94] It would, however, be far better to begin from one's present condition and from there seek the Lord's wisdom in how most effectively to approach and resolve their dysphoria.[95]

---

[92] See chapter 3, "Philosophical, Theological, and Historical Foundations of Transgender Identity."

[93] Isaiah 55:11

[94] https://transblog.grieve-smith.com/2019/08/ accessed December 5, 2019

[95] Granted, there are millions, perhaps as high as 1 in 1,500 births, born with abnormal

There is no specific marker, biological or otherwise, that clearly indicates if an individual is transgender. It is a matter of individual choice that occurs within one's mind. It is a personal perception. That decision is influenced, among other things, by one's upbringing, environment, personality, relationships, and attitude. If it is a matter of choice precipitated by external and internal social, emotional, and psychological influences, as argued in the chapter titled "Scientific Evidence Regarding Gender Dysphoria, Transgender, and Transsexual Identity," then there is no definitive physical baseline upon which to determine whether a person is transgender. Hence, for all practical purposes, it is a psychological construct, not a biological but a sociopsychological phenomenon. Since the entire concept of transgender identity is a social construct, one may hold to it with varying degrees. Some may be half-hearted and indecisive about it, while others may be confident and tenacious.

Yet all of this begs the question: If God is perfect and makes no mistakes, then why do some people believe that their physical bodies do not match their mental perception? One argument used quite effectively by many gender nonconformists is that they tend to feel trapped in a body that does not reflect their particular mind-set. They express the notion that if their outward appearance was altered, they would then have a greater opportunity for happiness. This type of thinking, albeit popular, is deeply flawed. A person's happiness is not contingent upon circumstances. It is an emotion over which one can opt either to experience and enjoy or reject. Frank Minirth and Paul Meyer penned a monograph in which they explained in detail how people may often fall into the trap of thinking that their happiness is somehow determined by extrinsic

---

genital makeup, but intersex individuals deserve their own separate discussion.

forces.[96] Nevertheless, the fact remains that happy people are those who choose to emulate that emotion. Happiness is determined by intrinsic rather than extrinsic forces. For instance, the Twelve Step Program, which has helped countless people face addictions and other personal problems, is based in large part on the concept that others, one's life circumstances, or any other external force can prompt or encourage negative or positive feelings, but one must make the final choice. No individual or thing can make anyone feel happiness. People choose how they feel. If one says that something or someone makes them happy or unhappy, what they really mean is that they choose to give to that person, event, or thing the power to determine how they feel. No one and nothing can force feelings upon a person. They were provided to humanity by the Creator, and through free will people choose which ones to adopt and hold sway. Often people will say that they only want their friends, family, colleagues, or associates to be happy, but happiness is not something that any individual can provide. Far better it is to inculcate others with the mind-set that they must choose to be happy. No one can or will provide it for them. Perhaps Solomon, the wisest person who ever lived, said it best: "For as he thinks within himself, so he is."[97]

In order to prevent some from taking major initiatives toward transitioning from one gender to another in a misguided quest for happiness, some experts in the field argue that there are certain steps that must be followed. Indeed, they desire to prevent any regrets regarding the so-called

---

[96] Frank Minirth and Paul Meyer. *Happiness is a Choice: New Ways to Enhance Joy and Meaning in Your Life, Revised and Expanded edition* (Baker Publishing House, February, 2013).

[97] Proverbs 23:7a

"sex reassignment surgery." For instance, the individual must live as the opposite sex for a significant amount of time, often one year, to see how they cope with the change. During this time hormonal and psychological therapy are geared toward adjustment into the new sex role. Furthermore, the person handles legal issues such as a name change and acquiring a new birth certificate. Many who specialize in this area have established other criteria that must be met in order to guarantee a successful transition into their new identities. The terms "sexual reassignment," "gender affirmation," or "gender confirmation" surgery are, at best, a misnomer. Chromosomally, nothing has changed. The person is still the same individual. A few anatomical changes do not make one male or female. The differences run far deeper than that.

Consider the trauma of the Ron and Janet Reimer family of Winnipeg, Manitoba. They had identical twin boys, Brian and Bruce, who were circumcised at several months of age. The botched procedure resulted in Bruce's genital mutilation. The parents heard psychologist Dr. John Money from Johns Hopkins University state that boys could be successfully reared as girls or vice versa and become well adapted to whatever sex they were taught to emulate. Hence, at two years of age, Bruce underwent sex reassignment surgery and became Brenda. It was succeeded by intensive therapy. Following puberty she began hormonal treatment until she was told the truth about her situation. Brenda hated life as a girl and was plagued with emotional, social, and psychological issues. When provided the opportunity Brenda became David and lived as a male until his untimely death, by suicide, in 2004.[98] Throughout his life David (Bruce/ Brenda) was always male in terms of his chromosomal makeup, mental

---

[98]   See *Sex: Unknown*, PBS NOVA original broadcast, October 30, 2001.

perception, and social experience. No amount of hormonal treatment, psychotherapy, surgical intervention, or rearing techniques could change the essential underlying reason for his maleness. He was formed in his mother's womb just like all humans to become the individual whom God determined.

When one considers the world's population, the large number of sperm a male produces during an average lifespan, along with the roughly 500 eggs a woman releases from the time of menarche to menopause, the odds of a specific man's individual sperm fertilizing a particular woman's precise egg is far beyond astronomical.[99] To deny any role that God plays in this is utter foolishness. One may read in Psalm 22:9–10 where David noted of the Father, "Yet You are He who brought me forth from the womb; You made me trust upon my mother's breasts. Upon You I was cast from birth; You have been my God from my mother's womb." Isaiah wrote roughly three centuries subsequent in 44:2: "Thus says the LORD who made you and formed you from the womb, who will help you, do not fear, O Jacob My servant; and you, Jeshurun whom I have chosen." Recall Jeremiah's words in 1:5: "Before I formed you in the womb I knew you, and before you were born I consecrated you; I have appointed you a prophet to the nations." In reference to Rebecca in Genesis 25:23, Moses authored, "The LORD said to her, 'Two nations are in your womb; and two peoples shall be separated from your body; and one people shall be stronger than the other; and the older shall serve the younger.'" Judge

---

[99]   A female is born with 1–2 million eggs, about 300,000 remain at puberty. A male produces roughly 500 billion sperm during an average lifespan.

Samson was "a Nazirite to God from the womb to the day of his death."[100] Job, in the midst of intense suffering, asked, "Did not He who made me in the womb make him, and in the same one fashion us in the womb?"[101] The beloved physician Luke recalled in his gospel in 1:15, referring to John the Baptist prior to his birth, "For he will be great in the sight of the Lord; and he will drink no wine or liquor, and he will be filled with the Holy Spirit while yet in his mother's womb." Paul communicated to the Galatians in 1:15–16a, "But when God, who had set me apart even from my mother's womb and called me through His grace, was pleased to reveal His Son in me so that I might preach Him among the Gentiles..." Scripture makes it quite apparent that prior to one's physical birth the Father knows everyone by name and has a course for their life. Most reject that plan by denying the Lord's offer of salvation.[102] Instead they exemplify Solomon's words: "There is a way which seems right to a man, but its end is the way of death."[103]

The Lord Jesus provides a clear example of this principle when He explains the parable of the sower. He stated, "When anyone hears the word of the kingdom and does not understand it, the evil one comes and snatches away what has been sown in his heart. This is the one on whom

---

[100] Judges 13:7c; see also Judges 16:17.

[101] Job 31:15

[102] In addressing the issue of salvation, Jesus stated in Matthew 7:13–14, "Enter through the narrow gate; for the gate is wide and the way is broad that leads to destruction, and there are many who enter through it. For the gate is small and the way is narrow that leads to life, and there are few who find it."

[103] Proverbs 16:25

seed was sown beside the road."[104] The first group describes those with no regard for Scripture, God, or anything related to Him. Indeed, they will often do what they can to frustrate the efforts of those whose lives are devoted to the Lord. Furthermore, they work diligently to prompt sociocultural acceptance of gender and sexual nonconformity, among other things. "The one on whom seed was sown on the rocky places, this is the man who hears the word and immediately receives it with joy; yet he has no firm root in himself but, is only temporary, and when affliction or persecution arises because of the word, immediately he falls away."[105] Sexual dysphoria and society's remedy often prompt those in this category to reject God as savior and choose the way that seems right to them. The Lord explained further in His parable: "And the one on whom seed was sown among the thorns, this is the man who hears the word, and the worry of the world and the deceitfulness of wealth choke the word, and it becomes unfruitful."[106] Those in this category make foolish choices by exposing themselves to unwise influences and associate with those obsessed with the temporal things of this world, including any type of non-biblically ordained sexual expression. When the eternal truth of the Word is rejected in favor of immediate gratification, outside influences hinder the truth from taking root. Thus a person in this category has at best an unfruitful life and, unlike Moses, chooses "to enjoy the passing pleasures of sin."[107] The Lord's parable concludes, "And the one on

---

[104] Matthew 13:19

[105] Matthew 13:20–21

[106] Matthew 13:22

[107] Hebrews 11:25b

whom seed was sown on the good soil, this is the man who hears the word and understands it; who brings forth, some a hundredfold, some sixty, and some thirty."[108] This is one who rejects the world's wisdom to accept their circumstances in order to find peace, fulfillment, contentment, and identity. Rather, they choose to accept their own sinfulness, confess, repent, and forsake it, and put their faith for eternal salvation in the Lord Jesus and find their true identity in Him. Moreover, they choose to renew their minds, focus on the Father, and live in complete obedience to Him. In short, they do not spend their lives for the present; they invest it for eternity.

Is acceptance truly the key for those who grieve from any form of non-biblical sexual expression among friends, family, associates, or other relationships? The scriptural answer is no. Inversely worldly wisdom contends that it is, and in many ways acknowledges a fatalistic attitude and approach toward life.[109] This certainly is not what Scripture teaches. "The LORD has established His throne in the heavens, and His sovereignty rules over all." The psalmist leaves no room for adopting a resigned or even defeatist perspective of any circumstances.[110] Rather, a much wiser approach to such situations is to seek the Lord through the Scripture to determine precisely what He is teaching.[111] The apostle Paul, in all

---

[108] Matthew 13:23

[109] It may indeed take some time to work through the grief. But to keep it from taking control, utilize the armor of God, as discussed in the chapter "Emotional Turmoil in Relational Transgender Identity."

[110] Psalm 103:19

[111] The chapter "Lessons from the Lord" provides insight into this process.

of his difficulties, certainly did not simply accept his thorn in the flesh. But after pleading for its removal learned that its purpose was for God's glory. Although he did not understand what had occurred to prompt his tremendous loss, Job did not accept it and find contentment. Rather, he questioned God, but when rebuked acknowledged the Father's sovereignty and was blessed abundantly. Moreover, in all of Holy Writ there is no acknowledgement of the legitimacy of non-biblical sexual expression. It is rather an example of sin and rebellion against nature and God Himself. Therefore follow the instruction found in Hebrews 4:16 and take that person "with confidence to the throne of grace...receive mercy and find grace to help in time of need."

CHAPTER 6

A PROBLEM OR
AN OPPORTUNITY FOR GROWTH?

Ho! Everyone who thirsts come to the waters; and you who have no money come, buy and eat. Come, buy wine and milk without money and without cost. Why do you spend money for what is not bread, and your wages for what does not satisfy? Listen carefully to Me, and eat what is good, and delight yourself in abundance. Incline your ear to Me. Listen, that you may live; and I will make an everlasting covenant with you, according to the faithful mercies shown to David.

ISAIAH 55:1–3

As one who is determined to bring division, grief, heartache, and destruction into evangelicals' lives, Satan often presents transgender identity as an insurmountable problem. For instance, certain parents may find it easier to disown their transgender child rather than to allow themselves to experience the intense pain, agony, and sense of loss it entails. Perhaps they may choose to shame and condemn their own flesh and blood. Family members, friends, or others may make a similar response. Some may take a biblical passage such as 2 Corinthians 6:17—which reads, "come out from their midst and be separate says the Lord"—to justify their brash behavior. Hence, a gigantic chasm emerges that might never be spanned. Any attempt to bridge the gap, no matter how well intentioned, will probably fail. Traditionally, problems were viewed as the final point of separation between two or more conflicting or even incompatible perspectives. It tended to prompt the assumption that, as a general rule, either one side or the other triumphed in the confrontation or perhaps the individuals compromised their positions to the point where no one was content. Yet it tends not to be helpful to incorporate such a rigid approach to scenarios similar to the one mentioned. Rather, it is incumbent that all consider seriously the words of Isaiah who wrote in 1:18, "'Come now, and let us reason together,' says the Lord, 'though your sins are as scarlet, they will be white as snow; though they are red like crimson, they will be like wool.'" Those who face disagreements regarding gender dysphoria, gender or sexual non-conformity, or anything similar would be wise as was the prophet to look for a resolution that honors the Father through the Son by the power of the Holy Spirit. Humbly seek His face; He can and will provide the necessary guidance.

The Bible provides a number of examples to illustrate this concept. Take, for instance, the account of the woman caught in adultery as recorded in John 8:3–12. The Scribes and the Pharisees brought her (the man somehow escaped, or at least is not mentioned) to Jesus. Mosaic law determined that both should be stoned, yet Roman law did not allow the death penalty in such a case. If she was stoned, the Scribes and the Pharisees seemingly triumphed and the Roman law was breached. If, on the other hand, she was not stoned, it appeared that Jesus promoted Roman over Moses' law. Essentially, one law would succeed and the other fail. However, the Lord's brilliant and unanticipated action illustrated a God-honoring response that was accepted and agreed to by all. He did not nullify Moses' command but ordered that the punishment be carried out by a sinless individual. He forced the accusers to examine themselves to see how well they kept the Mosaic regulations. Clearly, no one fit the description of being without sin, so no one could cast a stone against her. When the Scribes and the Pharisees departed, the Lord, who was perfect, forgave her and provided an opportunity for repentance. Indeed, Christ did not simply overlook her action. This was a profound resolution, because it forced everyone involved—the Scribes, the Pharisees, and the woman—to examine their behaviors closely and assess themselves individually. The Father holds us personally responsible to Himself for our own conversation, conduct, and character. Neither of the two seemingly obvious choices would have permitted such a thought-provoking and mindful self-evaluation of all involved. In essence, the third option reaped benefits for everyone. When family members, friends, associates, or others observe one of their own involved in unbiblical behavior that dishonors the Lord Jesus, it is easy to assume the role of Scribes and Pharisees as in the case of the woman caught in adultery. Yet the Lord does not want believers to justify their actions but to open their spiritual hearts, minds, and eyes to the truth that all have sinned and fall short of the glory of God. He wants all people to confess to Him of their own sinful attitudes and actions. Furthermore, He longs for their complete submission to Him. Just as He allowed the situation with the woman to teach her and the religious leaders a crucial truth, He desires for believers not to condemn but to confess their own rebellion and meditate on how best to point others to the Savior.

A second instance is recorded in Matthew 22:16–23, which focuses on the issue of remitting taxes. Herodians, in an attempt to trap Jesus, asked Him if it was lawful to pay a poll tax to Caesar. Their puerile minds expected a simple yes or no answer, either of which would place Jesus in an untenable position. If he agreed, it would undermine his propriety among many people who detested remitting Rome's levies to the tax collectors, who themselves were viewed by most Jews as traitors. But if the Lord protested the payments, He would jeopardize his position with Roman authorities. He acknowledged Caesar's inscription on the coin, hence his sanction. Therefore, Christ's response, "render to Caesar the things that are Caesar's; and to God the things that are God's," was an unexpected reply.[112] It did, however, recognize the validity of both Roman authority and the Father's ownership; hence, the solution was clearly accepted by all and honored God.

A third scenario is located in Luke 15:11–32, where we read the parable of the lost son. The younger of two sons asked for and received his share of the inheritance and wasted it on riotous, profligate, and unsavory living. In time he came to himself and returned to his father a humiliated and broken man seeking employment as a servant. The father was faced with the decision of disowning his son (as many Jewish fathers would have done) or hiring him as a servant. Note that the father did neither, nor did he contemplate either option. Rather, he opened his arms and

---

[112] Matthew 22:21b.

gladly restored him to his prior position. Both the father and his son could rejoice in this resolution. One may ask about the elder brother's attitude toward his dad's decision, but we must recall that the father reminded his firstborn that he had access to what his brother received; he simply never requested it.

The point manifested by these three examples is that when dealing with one experiencing gender dysphoria or sexual non-conformity of some kind, family, friends, acquaintances, and others should not view this as an either/or scenario. It is best not to reject the individual, but neither do we function as though it precipitated no change in the person. When all seek the Lord's rather than worldly human guidance and intervention, He can and will provide solutions not normally considered by those affected. So, rather than follow Satan's path that promotes division, animosity, resentment, and bitterness, diligently pursue from our sovereign Lord what other options are available. It is essential to spend time alone with Him, seek His face, feed and meditate on His Word, take any requests boldly to the Throne of Grace, listen for His wisdom and direction, and implement His resolution with integrity. Moreover, friends, acquaintances, family members, and others would be wise to research the issue of transgender identity so as to become better equipped to broach the topic and maintain positive relationships. It is a sad commentary indeed when something like this creates mayhem, mistrust, and disharmony among and within close relationships or families. To be sure, there are undoubtedly many instances where it may not be wise or even safe to pursue conflict resolution. Furthermore, the consequences of such action may have long-term negative ramifications. Thus, it is imperative to discern precisely the Lord's will and direction without relying upon any preconceived notions about what, if any action should be undertaken. Moving ahead without the Father's leadership is a recipe for disaster and may well make an exceptionally challenging situation considerably worse.

If the Lord gives a clear and unmistakable message to resolve the cognitive dissonance associated with incompatible positions, it is time to seek His wisdom from the Bible. For instance, while at Athens, Paul sought to lead people to the Lord, "so he was reasoning in the synagogue with the Jews and the God-fearing Gentiles, and in the marketplace every day with those who happened to be present."[113] In this discussion, reasoning is the operative term. Condemning one another, making unfounded accusations and generalizations, and acting in the flesh serve no edifying purpose. Uttering insults at someone is not helpful and should be avoided. Vitriolic confrontations merely intensify a difficult situation. It will not result in a plausible position for either party and certainly brings no honor to the Father, the Son, or the Holy Spirit. Indeed, it illustrates clearly that neither party is interested in seeking the Lord's direction in a precarious situation. It demonstrates however that all involved are determined to exacerbate an unhealthy and volatile scenario. The division rapidly turns into a gargantuan chasm which is exactly what the wicked one wants.

As the parties meet and converse, all involved must define the opposing ideologies that initially prompted the division. Although an observer may determine the existence only of preclusive positions, there is often much more than meets the eye. It can, for instance, be helpful for all to consider everyone's personal issues, traits, and persona as an iceberg. What others observe in one's life, the part above the water, is roughly

---

[113] Acts 17:17.

one-eighth of the individual. Hence, the vast majority lurks unseen beneath the surface. The visual component reflects only a small fraction of the individual's uniqueness. For example, the bulk of their experiences, perceptions, attitudes, worldview, beliefs, self-esteem, unresolved emotional issues, expectations, and desires remain hidden or unseen. Indeed, many people are probably unaware of the information that lurks within. The person we see, hear, or touch is often based primarily upon the visible components of one's entire personality.[114] An associate may sense some underlying issues but is unaware of their source. Thus, by making a decision based upon what is recorded by our sensory perceptions, one ignores the vast majority of a person's mental, social, physical, spiritual, and emotional makeup. It may therefore be, indeed probably is, inaccurate. People may not truly understand why they think as they do, why certain things bother them, or what prompts sensitivity to various issues. In fact, the transgender is probably unaware of what initially prompted his or her sexual dysphoria. Often this condition leads to a person's desire for acceptance or approval and results in rebellion along with its highly destructive behavior. How then, one might ask, can a person become apprised of these hidden traits? Remember that the Father knows each person better than that individual knows herself or himself. He can and will reveal the information. One needs to turn to Him to secure the answer. Seek His solutions rather than turning to the world's remedies. Recall, for instance, the prophet Jeremiah's words in 17:9–10, "The heart is more deceitful than all else and is desperately sick; who can understand it? I the Lord

---

[114] Barry L. Reece, Monique E. Reece, *Effective Human Relations, 13th ed.* Boston: Cengage Learning, 2017, 281–295.

search the heart, I test the mind, even to give to each man according to his ways, according to the results of his deeds."

Another issue that needs to be addressed regarding an opportunity for growth is the entire question of the role sexuality plays in our personhood. Scripture is quite clear in its description of male and female. Genesis 1:27 reads, "So God created man in His own image, in the image of God He created him; male and female he created them." The subsequent verse continues, "God blessed them; and God said to them, 'Be fruitful and multiply, and fill the earth, and subdue it....'" Thus, we have the two sexes through which procreation is made possible. Moreover, in Genesis 2:7, we read a more detailed account of Adam's creation: "Then the Lord God formed man of dust from the ground, and breathed into his nostrils the breath of life; and man became a living being." In verse 18, "God said, 'It is not good for the man to be alone; I will make him a helper suitable for him.'" Later we learn that "God fashioned into a woman the rib from which He had taken from the man and brought her to the man. The man said, 'This is now bone of my bones, and flesh of my flesh; she shall be called Woman because she was taken out of Man.'" God clearly stated that she was a helper suitable for him. Neither sex was to control or dominate the other; rather they were to complement each other, male and female.

God is clearly relational. Indeed, He is the Creator and Sustainer of the universe. He was crucified on the cross, buried, and rose from the dead. Furthermore, He indwells believers, as Paul relates we are the temple of the Holy Spirit. The Trinity is comprised of one God who is three distinct persons. Humans are created in His image. Following nearly every component of creation, God said that it was good. However, in Genesis 1:31

succeeding the creation of humanity, the Holy Writ reads, "And God saw all that He had made and behold it was very good. And there was evening and there was morning the sixth day." Only after the creation of humanity did He include the amplifier "very" to the descriptor "good." Just as God provided humans with emotions, personalities, and other non-visual components, He also included sexuality, male and female. In Genesis 2, Scripture expounds upon God's creation of humanity. Adam was formed initially, but in verse 18, the Creator noted, "It is not good for the man to be alone; I will make him a helper suitable for him." The Hebrew word translated suitable, *neged*, means opposite or counterpart, or in this context, complementary. Thus, the two will work together nicely as partners. Following Eve's creation in Genesis 2, the Bible reads in verse 24, "For this reason a man shall leave his father and his mother, and be joined to his wife; and they shall become one flesh."

God is involved in relationships. He never intended for humans to function alone. Galatians 6:2 reads, "Bear one another's burdens, and thereby fulfill the law of Christ." In 1 Thessalonians 3:2–3, Paul relates that he and Silvanus "sent Timothy, our brother and minister of God, and our fellow laborer in the gospel of Christ to establish you and encourage you concerning your faith, that no one should be shaken by these afflictions; for you yourselves know that we are appointed to this." The three persons of the Godhead are fully complementary; the Father, the Son, and the Holy Spirit at some point before the foundation of the world determined the method of salvation. The Son would become sin and make possible the means of atonement for humanity, but each individual must choose to accept the Son's payment for their own personal sin debt. The Father agreed to accept the Son's crucifixion and shed blood for that atonement.

The Holy Spirit accepted responsibility to bring conviction to individuals for their sin and their need to trust personally the Savior's sacrifice. He also seals believers unto the day of redemption. The three persons of the Trinity perform many other functions as well, but the point here is to demonstrate how they mesh together in perfect congruence to accomplish the work of salvation.

Just as the Triune God works in complete harmony, so too are men and women to work in sync. But in the Garden of Eden, Satan entered into the picture and sin disrupted the perfect plan that God ordained. In our fallen condition, two crucial sexual characteristics, femininity and masculinity, became tainted and continue to this day on their destructive path. Too many believers who study the Bible diligently and seek to honor Him with their lives are dragged into this deep, ugly, God-dishonoring morass. The man and woman enjoyed unspoiled fellowship with each other and with God. Indeed, humans were created to be in relationship. The perfection of humanity was reflected in this connection. Everything was based on their position with God. He had given instructions to Adam as noted in Genesis 2:16–17. For his own protection, Adam was warned not to eat of the fruit of the tree of the knowledge of good and evil. When Satan appears in Genesis 3:1–3, the reader realizes that Adam had communicated that same information to Eve. Although whether he told her not to touch the fruit, we are unaware.

We do know, however, that both consumed the forbidden fruit and sin entered into the world. Perhaps the most tragic consequence of that action was the broken relationship between God and humanity as well as its disintegration between Adam and Eve. Where they once thrived in perfect union with one specific purpose, to live in complete connectivity with their creator and each other, division, fear, and a host of other God-dishonoring traits emerged. A deeper study of this event may provide helpful insight into the scenario regarding humanity.

A primary component of maleness is masculinity, while its counterpart, femaleness, is femininity. These complementary aspects of human sexuality are crucial in developing an accurate understanding of humanity. However, the world's (non-biblical) viewpoint created a false understanding of masculinity and femininity that permeates much of society. For instance, some occupations that require intense physical labor may be described as masculine while other vocations which necessitate tender loving care are deemed feminine. This false dichotomy is certainly not found in Holy Writ and often leads to discord and confusion. Moreover, stereotypes frequently emerge, which merely confound the convolution. Since the advent of sin, the fallen nature has contrived a perception of masculinity and femininity without a biblical foundation. This tainted understanding has permeated much of society. The two traits that were designed primarily to affect how an individual relates with God and others as the Creator intended became essentially a false comparison between men and women. What the Creator designed to complement relationships became instead Satan's substitute that caused division, heartbreak, and loneliness.

However, an in-depth study and analysis of the original biblical language provides a clearer scriptural perspective for what Godly masculinity and femininity entails. If we examine the biblical text regarding creation, it becomes evident what the Creator had in mind for men and women. The book of Genesis was written in ancient Hebrew, a language with which very few are acquainted, thus necessitating its translation into more common vernaculars. This challenging process can alter the author's original intent to the degree that much of the meaning is lost. Words can have connotations and implications in the original that are not present in the newer languages, and vice versa. The concepts of masculinity and femininity are a case in point. In the account of creation, this dilemma arises. Note several words that illustrate this contention. The first is located in Genesis 1:26, "Then God said, 'Let Us make man in our image, according to Our likeness and let them rule over the fish of the sea and over the birds of the sky and over the cattle and over all the earth, and over every creeping thing that creeps on the earth." The word translated man is the Hebrew word *adam*. It means a person or individual but does not specify man or woman; Scripture here refers to a human being.[115]

The subsequent verse, 27, utilizes another helpful word for this discussion. Scripture reads "God created man in His own image, in the image of God He created him; male and female He created them." The term translated image is *tselem*, which means illusion, phantom, or resemblance.[116] In this context, we see that humans are not a physical representation of God, but are more spiritual in nature as the terms phantom and illusion imply. There is the physical component of creation, but humans received other aspects as well such as soul and spirit, as discussed later in the chapter. Moreover, as God is one in three persons with perfect relational

---

[115] Larry Crabb, *Fully Alive: A Biblical Vision of Gender that Frees Men and Women to Live Beyond Stereotypes*, (Grand Rapids: Baker Books, 2013), 38.

[116] See James Strong, *Strong's Exhaustive Concordance*, (Nashville: Abingdon Press, 1974, 32nd printing) and Jay P. Green, ed. *The Interlinear Hebrew-Greek-English Bible*, 2nd ed. (Peabody: Hendrickson Publishers, 1985 reprint 2007) for helpful insight into definitions and specific nuances in Scripture's original languages.

oneness, so is His intention for humans. Indeed, the Hebrew word for God here is *Elohim*, a plural term that can imply the three persons of the Godhead.

An examination of Genesis 2:23–24 introduces two more words for study. "The man said, 'This is now bone of my bones and flesh of my flesh; she shall be called Woman because she was taken out of Man.' For this reason a man shall leave his father and his mother, and be joined to his wife; and they shall become one flesh." Woman is translated from the Hebrew word *ishshah*, which can also mean wife. *Iysh* is rendered man in verse 24, but it can also mean husband. Thus, we see that *adam* means individual or person, *ishshah* is the word for woman while *iysh* is man. Interestingly, *iysh* is translated manchild in Genesis 4:1, noting that Cain's anatomy reflected his father's. There is no notion of gender, but there are clearly two sexes which comprise humanity.[117]

Genesis 1:27 is the next verse under this examination of Hebrew terminology. "God created man in His own image, in the image of God he created him; male and female He created them." Here the Bible introduces the concept of gender with two terms, *zakar* and *neqebah*. *Zakar*, for instance, is translated male and means memorable, moving, or action. In the Ancient Near East, *zakar* could be described as a man who reminded an individual of, say, an appointment and did what was necessary to cause it to occur. Masculinity reflects the idea of reminding others of truth along with an action that promotes what is memorable.

Larry Crabb insightfully describes Godly masculinity. When a man hears and responds to others in need, he remembers the God he is called to reveal by his conduct, conversation, and character. A masculine man

---

[117] Crabb, *Fully Alive,* 39–40.

sees others in distress and remembers that the ideal assistance he can provide is to offer the presence of Christ. A masculine man moves to assist others to reveal not his own personal strength but to demonstrate God's character and to point them toward the master. Relational masculinity is reflected in a man who remembers God's story and acts in ways to fulfill its plot.[118] Note that relational, Godly, or biblical masculinity puts the emphasis not on self but on the Master Himself. It is selflessness. Worldly, ungodly, and non-scriptural masculinity focuses entirely on self. It is complete selfishness.

Similarly, *neqebah* reflects a woman, designed to invite, not to control or demand. Further, the word implies someone with a discerning spirit. Femininity, then, is defined as a judicious woman who is willing to invite and encourage others, not to direct or dominate them. Crabb contends that a feminine woman is an inviter, not a controller or manipulator. A feminine woman is perceptive and receives only what reflects God's character and furthers His purpose. Relational femininity runs in two directions: an openness to receive and a willingness to give.[119] Godly, relational, biblical femininity directs one's attention to God, not oneself. It is selfless. However, worldly, ungodly, and non-biblical femininity draws attention to oneself. It is selfishness.

One more Hebrew word is quite helpful in this study on femininity and masculinity. This is an often misunderstood term and many are led astray because few English translations provide an accurate understanding of the author's intent. Genesis 3:16 reads: "To the woman He said,

---

[118] Crabb, *Fully Alive,* 72–78.

[119] Crabb, *Fully Alive,* 41–47.

'I will greatly multiply your pain in childbirth, in pain you shall bring forth children; yet your desire shall be for your husband, and he shall rule over you." The word under consideration, *teshuwqah*, is translated desire. Many have implied that in His rebuke, God tells the woman she is to desire her husband. That may be a popular understanding of the verse, but it is not without considerable controversy.

Susan T. Foh authored a highly influential article in 1975 titled, "What is the Woman's Desire?" Prior to Foh's work, most interpreted the verse as "an instruction to desire her husband who ruled over her." She, however, in a response to feminism in Scripture, analyzed the passage with astute insight and acumen. The term *teshuwqah* is found in only two more verses. One is in the Song of Solomon 4:7, but it is probably more helpful to use the third location, Genesis 4:7, because it was written by the same individual in the same book as the initial example. Indeed, hermeneutics explains that the best and most effective means of understanding a biblical term is to examine its usage in a nearby location. Through a close comparison between these two examples, Foh arrived at her conclusion.[120] Genesis 4:7 reads: "If you do well, will not your countenance be lifted up? And if you do not do well, sin is crouching at the door, and its desire is for you, but you must master it." As God conversed with Cain, He related that sin's desire was to control him. And indeed it did as in the next verse we read that Cain murdered his brother Abel. Just as sin's desire was to dominate Cain, after the fall Eve's desire was to control and dominate Adam. Thus, the pure sinless concept of femininity, including discernment, openness and giving to complement masculine traits

---

[120] Susan T. Foh, "What is the Woman's Desire?" *The Westminster Theological Journal 37* (1974–75) pp. 376–83.

of recalling, reminding what is memorable and acting toward that end became tainted and competitive.[121]

An examination of Adam and Eve's actions reveals how quickly the sin-spoiled version of masculinity and femininity entered the world. In Genesis 3:6 we read, "When the woman saw that the tree was good for food, and that it was a delight to the eyes, and that the tree was desirable to make one wise, she took from its fruit and ate; and she gave also to her husband with her, and he ate." If Adam had demonstrated relational masculinity, he would have recalled the specific instructions given to him regarding that fruit, warned Eve of the consequences and pointed her toward the Creator, but he refused to fulfill his biblical obligation. The apostle Paul penned in Romans 5:12, "Therefore, just as through one man sin entered into the world, and so death spread to all men, because all sinned...." The Greek word translated man is *anthropos* and in this context refers not to humanity but to a specific male, Adam. Moreover, the means by which sin entered was not necessarily an action on his part but could have occurred by observation. Thus, it is highly plausible that God viewed Adam's refusal to prevent Eve from her action as the means by which sin entered the world. She then lost Godly femininity with its openness, giving, and discernment but obtained the desire to control her husband. He did not fulfill his responsibilities, so she was going to do it for him.

---

[121] Complementarians and others have eagerly utilized Foh's understanding even to the point that it is now perhaps among the most widely accepted interpretation of Genesis 3:16. Indeed, her understanding of the verse is found in the *New Living Translation*. For a fuller study of this intriguing study, see Susan T. Foh, *Woman and the Word of God: A Response to Biblical Feminism, 2nd ed.* (Grand Rapids: Baker Books, 1981).

An analysis of several biblical characters comparing the worldly and biblical perspectives may be helpful to reflect this point. For example, Adam and Eve's first two children, Cain and Abel, had different occupations. Cain was a tiller of the ground while Abel kept sheep. Initially, one might determine that both were highly masculine, but a closer examination requires a more complex investigation. The world might determine that farming was perhaps more masculine than shepherding since God's Word describes various shepherdesses, such as Rachel as seen in Genesis 29:9, Moses' wife Zipporah and her sisters as noted in Exodus 2:16–21, as well as the Shulamite woman discussed in the Song of Solomon 1:7–8. We are, however, greatly challenged to find as many women who tilled the soil. Granted, Ruth gleaned wheat and barley, but we read of fewer who worked the land than of those who kept the flocks. Both shepherding and farming required considerable physical strength and stamina, and both men and women are recorded as doing the work, so we cannot place either of those tasks as purely masculine or feminine. A biblical understanding, however, conveys that one's occupation does not determine their femininity or masculinity. Femininity requires discernment, openness, and giving, traits found in Rachel, Zipporah, the Shulamite woman, and Ruth. Abel was most definitely masculine as he remembered the requirements for an offering to the Lord and he fulfilled his responsibility, contrary to his brother.

A cursory examination of Cain's genealogy reveals the sons of Lamech in Genesis 4:20–22. Jabal became the father of those who lived in tents and kept livestock, yet his brother Jubal's line included all those who played the harp and flute. Finally, Tubal-Cain was an instructor of craftsmen in iron and bronze. Sin-tainted culture may perhaps contend that Jubal's occupation had both masculine and feminine characteristics, such as the case with Tubal-Cain. In 1 Kings 1:40, at the anointing of King Solomon, Scripture states: "And all the people went up after him, and the people were playing on flutes and rejoicing with great joy, so that the earth shook at their noise." All the people undoubtedly signifies both men and women; hence, one cannot say that playing a musical instrument is purely feminine or masculine. However, the Bible imparts that believers are to honor the Lord. Recalling that fact and bringing it to fruition reflects biblical masculinity while discerning women opening themselves up to encourage others and point them to the Savior is femininity at its apex.

Later in Genesis, we read of Isaac's and Rebekah's twin sons, Esau and Jacob. Genesis 25:27 tells us that Esau was a skillful hunter, a man of the field, while Jacob was a mild man dwelling in tents. The world says that Esau was the quintessential example of a "man's man," hairy and overflowing with testosterone. But we know that he also cooked as he prepared his game as his father requested before providing the blessing. Yet Jacob was more interested in seemingly feminine pursuits such as cooking and other related domestic tasks. But he became the father of Israel's twelve tribes. So, we see the confusion as noted earlier: Were these men masculine? Were they feminine? Using the world's standards, how can one know? But with a Godly understanding, we see that Esau certainly did not represent masculinity as he traded his birthright for a bowl of soup. He did not recall how important and memorable was his familial position as the eldest son and he let it go. Jacob, on the other hand, with the Lord's guidance, grew in his ability to recall his God and spent his life serving the Lord. His masculinity is not in doubt.

Jesus himself was a carpenter, a typically masculine occupation, yet during His ministry He pursued more of what society might define as feminine tasks such as teaching the people, spending time with children, and dealing with people in an overtly loving but firm manner. Thus, a worldly view leaves one perplexed regarding His masculinity and femininity. Mark 14:36 reads, "And as He was saying, 'Abba! Father! All things are possible for You; remove this cup from Me; yet not what I will, but what You will." He remembered His mission and willingly went to the cross to carry it out. His action is probably the strongest example of biblical masculinity.

Paul, the great missionary, was trained as a Pharisee, yet he was also a tentmaker, a trade he undoubtedly learned while apprenticed as a youth. It necessitated great skill and precision in stitching, cutting, and working with various fabrics. However, after he converted and became essentially a self-funded missionary through his portable occupation, he reflected a man of enormous strength and stamina. Beginning in 2 Corinthians 11:24–25, Paul wrote, "Five times I received from the Jews 39 lashes. Three times I was beaten with rods, once I was stoned, three times I was shipwrecked, a night and a day I have spent in the deep." These clearly do not reflect a physically feeble man. His incredible strength was necessary for survival. The apostles John and Peter were strong fishermen, bold and impetuous. Yet they also wrote several books of Holy Writ that reflect a spirit of tenderness and mercy. The masculine Paul never forgot His Savior and his life was spent honoring Him and pointing others toward salvation. The same may be said for John and Peter.

One may also find women who appeared to demonstrate both masculinity and femininity in their lives. For instance, we read in Judges 4 that Deborah served as a judge to the children of Israel, and because of Barak's cowardice she successfully led the Hebrew forces against the Canaanites. Yet afterward, she composed and sang a song honoring God for His great victory. Esther was a beautiful and feminine woman whom Ahasuerus selected as the queen of Persia. She exhibited numerous traits of womanhood. However, when her people were sold to destruction, she willingly approached the king at the risk of her own immediate execution to bring the matter to his attention. Furthermore, she confronted Haman, the king's second in command, and the source of the Jews' dilemma. Both of these women were quintessential examples of discerning individuals who opened themselves up to encourage others and point them toward the Savior.

All of these biblical examples describe numerous men and women who visibly demonstrated what the world would perhaps describe as both feminine and masculine traits. Yet when examined under the microscope of Scripture, it becomes apparent that the truly Godly women demon-strated femininity while their male counterparts illustrated masculinity. Granted, individuals are typically born with the XX or XY chromosome, which cannot be changed. Physically, people are male or female with the rare exception of those who are to one degree or another hermaphroditic or intersex. Although they deserve considerable treatment, it is beyond the scope of this piece.

The discussion of masculinity and femininity according to a popular but non-biblical mindset raises no fewer than three problematic com-ponents. What some highly influential social movers and shakers have erroneously contended is that if an individual's biological makeup is, say, male but they tend toward more female characteristics according to the worldly definition, that person will not feel happy or fulfilled until their "biological sex" equates with their mental, intellectual, emotional, and social sex. If one's emotional traits equal their physical traits, then they will feel more at home with their own body and find a greater degree of freedom. No longer would they sense a gap between their emotional and biological makeup. They would in fact find happiness and no longer face this dualistic struggle that appears to cause so much internal strife and external duress. By the same token, women who express the world's perception of masculinity could secure that same sense of internal peace, security, and happiness by "becoming" a man. The notion of altering one's sex, however logical it may sound, is deeply flawed. It clearly makes numerous inaccurate presuppositions; perhaps the most egregious is that it neglects the biblical understanding of womanhood, femininity, manhood, and masculinity.

A second issue is that people are not comprised of two elements. Some Dualists contend that people have a non-physical component comprised of mind, emotions, and personality, all of which are unseen. Secondly, they have a physical or visible element, their body. Most who cling to this erroneous perception tend to accept that at physical death a person ceases to exist, there is not an eternal afterlife.[122] Although that presupposition is popular, Scripture clearly indicates that trialism is more accurate.[123] All

---

[122] Dualism has many applications in disciplines such as psychology, sociology, philosophy, religion, and law. This discussion refers to the general concept of human dualism, mind (*psyche*) and body (*soma*), as espoused by Rene Descartes and others.

[123] See, for example, Genesis 7 which reads: "Then the LORD God formed man of dust from the ground, and breathed into his nostrils the breath of life and man became a living being." Formed is from *yetsur* which often describes a potter and clay, hence the physical component. Breathed indicates the soul while *hayah,* translated became,

have a body (physical), soul (personality, mind), and spirit (the eternal component). Moreover, minds incorporate intellect, emotion, and will. An examination of people's intricacies makes it apparent that humans are far more complex than some contend and believe. A person's perception of their femininity or masculinity falls under the soul or emotional component. Hence, it occupies only one of the three divisions that comprise an individual. Hence, far too much emphasis is placed on those characteristics. Indeed, if one supposedly plumbs biological and mental sex (otherwise known as gender reassignment or gender conforming surgery), other categories of our humanity are not necessarily in line.

A remaining issue to consider is one's identity. If someone introduces themselves, they typically explain who they are; most non-believers would address topics such as occupation, interests, likes/dislikes, family, experiences, education, and perhaps political views. A person's sexuality is rarely in the mix. This is not to say that it does not occur, but the exceptions are highly uncommon. Yet for a believer, what is their true identity? In 1 Corinthians 6:20 and 7:23, God's Word demonstrates that "we are not our own, but we were bought with a price." Paul relates in 2 Corinthians 5:21 that "He made Him who knew no sin, to be sin on our behalf that we might become the righteousness of God in Him." In other words, while

---

infers to cause something to occur. The living being is the man's spirit. Paul reiterates this in 1 Thessalonians 5:23 where he writes: "Now may the God of peace Himself sanctify you entirely and may your spirit and soul and body be preserved complete, without blame at the coming of our Lord Jesus Christ. The author of Hebrews concurs in 4:12 which reads: "For the word of God is active and sharper than any two edged sword, and piercing as far as the division of soul and spirit, of joint and marrow, and able to judge the thoughts and intentions of the heart. Soul, spirit, joints and marrow refer to the three basic components of a human.

on the cross, Jesus not only carried all the sin of the world but actually became sin as well so that when He died, the power of sin perished. Thus, believers are Christ's righteousness. In Galatians 2:20, Paul writes, "I have been crucified with Christ; and it is no longer I who live, but Christ lives in me; and the life which I now live in the flesh I live by faith in the Son of God, who loved me and gave Himself up for me." Those who personally confess their sins to the Father and accept the Lord Jesus into their heart are empowered by the Spirit who gives life. Indeed, the same idea of God breathing into Adam the breath of life was present when the Holy Spirit was breathed into new believers. The word translated "breath" in Genesis 2:7 comes from the Hebrew word *neshamah*, which can mean inspiration, soul or spirit, the components of life. In Luke's description of Pentecost in Acts 2:4a, we read, "And they were all filled with the Holy Spirit." The word filled is translated from the Greek *pletho*, which incorporates the idea of fulfill, accomplish, or even perhaps furnish. A component of salvation is that it includes the Holy Spirit entering into and indwelling believers; indeed, Paul wrote in 1 Corinthians 6:19–20, "Do you not know that your body is a temple of the Holy Spirit who is in you, whom you have from God, and that you are not your own? For you have been bought with a price: therefore glorify God in your body." As He indwells saints, He empowers them to live in obedience to Him.

In his gospel, the apostle John explained in the first few verses of chapter 15 that He is the vine and Christians are the branches. As believers abide in Him, He abides in them. John 14:23 reads, "If anyone loves Me he will keep My word; and My Father will love him, and We will come to him and make Our abode with him." Hence, a surface examination of the Bible indicates clearly that believers, those who have trusted in Christ's sacrificial death on the cross alone as payment for their sin debt in full, are indwelt by the Father, the Son, and the Holy Spirit. While incarcerated in Rome, Paul related in Ephesians 2:10a that "we are His workmanship, created in Christ Jesus." Even the prophet Jeremiah wrote in 1:5, "Before I formed you in the womb I knew you, and before you were born I consecrated you: I have appointed you a prophet to the nations." Isaiah authored similarly in 44:2, "Thus says the Lord who made you and formed you from the womb,..." Hence, believers can understand clearly that their identity is inextricably interwoven with the Lord's. Furthermore, it begins long before one's physical birth. Statements such as when a young four-year-old boy named Nick told his mother, "God made a mistake, and that he should have been made a girl," are incompatible with a biblical worldview.[124] First of all, God does not make mistakes. Secondly, He has a plan for everyone; that they should come to a saving knowledge of Christ. The succeeding component is that believers are to be conformed to the image of His Son. Indeed, David's comments in Psalm 139:15–16 enlighten and comfort: "My frame was not hidden from You, when I was made in secret, and skillfully wrought in the depths of the earth; Your eyes have seen my unformed substance; and in Your book were all written the days that were ordained for me, when as yet there was not one of them." Such words certainly do not reflect One who errs. Transgender identity, transsexual identity gender dysphoria, and other related disorders are certainly not part of His Will. One may feel strongly that God allows and perhaps even sanctions that they are, but it certainly contradicts His Word. Moreover, putting one's trust in the emotions and ideas that prompt and fuel such behavior is a dangerous, if not deadly, path as noted in a previous chapter.

---

[124] Rachel Pepper, 92.

Clearly, one's sexuality is an important part of human identity. Indeed on more than one occasion God instructed His people to be fruitful and multiply. However, sexuality is merely one component among many. Moreover, since humans were formed by the Creator, it is, to say the least, highly presumptuous to present oneself as variant from what God determined. By examining God's Word, seeking His guidance, and obeying the Holy Spirit's promptings, one can truly allow Him to transform what many perceive as a problem into a vibrant opportunity for spiritual growth. Through an examination of issues such as masculinity and femininity along with an exploration of what truly makes people human, it becomes obvious that sexuality is not the primary contributing factor to a person's identity. Believers belong to Christ, He lives in and through them as they open themselves to Him. By allowing Him to work on their mindset, attitudes, conduct, conversations, and character, they become more like the One who created humanity, died for them, and indwells those who trust Him as their Savior. All of which should strengthen one's walk with the Lord, facilitating a deep, personal, intimate, and growing relationship with Him. Granted, the transgender may reject any and all of these truths. Nevertheless, the Lord can and will use the experiences of relational transgender identity to enhance one's own personal journey with Him.

CHAPTER 7

EFFECTIVE COMMUNICATION: NECESSARY FOR RELATIONSHIP

> "For I know the plans that I have for you," declares the Lord, "plans for welfare and not for calamity to give you a future and a hope. Then you will call upon Me and come and pray to Me, and I will listen to you. You will seek Me and find Me when you search for Me with all your heart."
>
> JEREMIAH 29:11–13

Communication is an essential component of any relationship. Without it, one cannot have a means of relaying interests, thoughts, feelings, ideas, or express other substantive information upon which any bond is based. If one's desire is to facilitate mutual transmission, he or she must be willing to exert considerable effort to develop, foster, and encourage it. When one examines what the Father did to reveal Himself to humanity, what the Son did on the cross to demonstrate His *agape*, and what the Holy Spirit does today, the lengths to which God goes to facilitate His communication with humanity become apparent. Clearly, God prioritizes interaction; it is critically important. Most humans reject His efforts, yet He continues because He is not willing that any perish but that all come to repentance. When considering the extent to which the Lord pursues contact with humanity, it is completely logical to presume that it should also be highly important for individuals. This is particularly true in challenging situations such as when dealing with a transgender, transsexual, gender fluid, gender or sexual non-conformist or gender dysphoria suffering friend, acquaintance, colleague, neighbor, or loved one.

Should one desire to resolve any difficulties with the relationship, the responsibility lies with the believer to enhance and facilitate communication. Granted, to many it may appear to be easier not to focus on maintaining contact but to wait for the transgender to reach out themself. However, since God so highly prioritizes relationships, believers should adopt a similar perspective. Yet this is premised on the assumption that it is safe to do so. There are undoubtedly myriad circumstances where pursuing interaction with that person or persons will be more detrimental or perhaps even harmful than helpful. Should that be the case, one would be foolish and asking for trouble to instigate or continue attempts at pursuing contact. Rather, take that person boldly to the throne of grace regularly and persistently and allow the Father, His Word, and His Spirit to tenderize their heart and open their mind that they might turn to Him in repentance. Be sensitive to the Spirit and His leading and obey Him. The clear biblical admonition is to remove oneself from hindering the Lord and allow the Holy Spirit to work in and through them to accomplish His objectives.

Some may be quick to jump to passages such as 2 Corinthians 6:17, which reads, "'Therefore, come out from their midst and be separate,' says the Lord. 'And do not touch what is unclean; and I will welcome you,'" to justify a termination of communication. Such behavior, however, is a potentially unhelpful response. A rudimentary contextual analysis of the apostle Paul's words provides keen insight into the matter. His Holy Spirit–breathed correspondence addressed a Church body that appeared to pride itself in opening the door toward promoting sexual behavior that was not seen even among unbelievers. A man and his stepmother lived as husband and wife. The Corinthians apparently tolerated, accepted, and approved of believers mocking the Lord's Supper, suing one another over various issues, and committing gross sexual immorality. The Lord instructed believers to disassociate themselves from such individuals to allow the Holy Spirit to bring conviction upon the ostracized and facilitate their confession, repentance, and forsaking of the sin. Essentially, the break in communication was designed to accomplish a God-honoring response on the part of the offending parties. The apostle did not eliminate contact for the purpose of placing himself or the Church in judgment of others, but rather to create an environment for all to focus on Christ and His atoning death on the cross. Thus, it is imperative to utilize communication to maintain an open door for mutual growth.

How do we accomplish such an overriding task, especially since in previous encounters the result prompted poor behavior and seemed to turn the relationship back? A major challenge for those who depend upon text messages, e-mails, Twitter, Facebook, LinkedIn, or any type of social media is to minimize dependence upon new technology for communication. Some find it so much more convenient to send an e-mail, text a message, or make a telephone call when a face-to-face session could prove much more effective and productive. The effort required to speak one on one is a clear indicator of a person's desire to maintain an open line of communication. Granted, that is not always possible, feasible, or even safe as previously noted; nevertheless, it is perhaps the optimum form of relating one to another. This may be particularly true if the relationship is damaged or even tenuous. It is incumbent to seek diligently the Lord's wisdom and obey His direction. Should God encourage the communication but it does not work to meet face-to-face, utilize the telephone or some form of one-on-one technology.

With the Scripture as one's guide, the Lord provides plenty of reasons to maintain communication along with the consequences of its neglect. Examine, for example, King David, a man after God's own heart. He most certainly was a great ruler who generally set a fine example for his subjects. However, his record as a familial communicator was not so stellar. Take, for instance, the situation discussed in 2 Samuel 11, when he took Bathsheba, Uriah's wife, as his own and had her husband murdered. Two heinous sins for which he repented, as recorded in Psalm 51 and elsewhere, but he experienced the consequences the rest of his days. One reads of an example described in 2 Samuel 13 and following. Amnon, the royal son, raped Tamar, his half-sister. In verse 21 "when David heard of all these matters he was very angry." Nevertheless, Holy Writ implies that David did not intervene. Indeed, with his adulterous and murderous behavior, how could he? Therefore, Absalom took it upon himself to avenge her by killing Amnon two years subsequent. He fled from his father, but David's love became apparent in verse 37, where God's Word tells us that "David mourned for his son every day." Absalom remained in exile for three years "and the heart of King David longed to go out to Absalom for he was comforted concerning Amnon since he was dead."[125]

The monarch could have communicated with his son during this time, but apparently because of his own sin, chose not to do so. It is perhaps speculation, but the chasm that emerged between Absalom and his father continued to widen and deepen. Finally, Joab, David's top general, recalled Absalom to Jerusalem, but David refused to see him. Absalom's father said regarding his son, "Let him turn to his own house and let him not see my face."[126] The king's son resided in Jerusalem for two years without seeing his dad. In other words, this family was so torn apart that father and son had no communication, verbal or otherwise, for five full years! This was not an effective strategy on David's part, since clearly he loved Absalom but certainly did not express it toward his son. What a terrible tragedy for that family, but the entire scenario continued to deteriorate. Finally Absalom, who communicated through Joab, convinced the general to influence the king for a meeting, so after half a decade had passed, Absalom "came to the king and prostrated himself on his face to the ground before the king, and the king kissed Absalom."[127] We are not informed of any more immediate communication between the two, but Scripture tells us that "Absalom said to the king, 'Please let me go and pay my vow which I have vowed to the Lord in Hebron.'"[128] David responded,

---

[125] 2 Samuel 13:38–39.

[126] 2 Samuel 14:24.

[127] 2 Samuel 14:33.

[128] 2 Samuel 15:7.

"Go in peace."[129] Absalom resided in Jerusalem at David's pleasure, so apparently his son felt it necessary to request permission to depart. The monarch was so clueless regarding Absalom's mindset that he apparently had no idea that his son left not to pay any vow, but to initiate a mass conspiracy that even included close associates such as the priest and confidant Ahithophel that nearly toppled David from power.

David's paternal love again rose to the surface as he communicated to his military leaders, "Deal gently for my sake with the young man Absalom." Joab, however, did not follow this instruction and killed the rebellious leader. In a telling time following Absalom's defeat and demise, David "was deeply moved.... And thus he said as he walked, 'O my son Absalom, my son, my son Absalom! Would I had died instead of you, O Absalom, my son, my son.'"[130] During the showdown between the two armies, Scripture records in 2 Samuel 18:7 that 20,000 combatants died. Hence, this family struggle resulted in the loss of many innocent Hebrews.

Clearly, we can never know how much of this long-lasting and deep-seated familial tragedy could have been averted if David had taken a more proactive rather than reactive role. However, there is little doubt that his non-interference was an ineffective strategy that served him, his family, his friends, and his kingdom poorly. Indeed, had David initiated interaction with his son, perhaps much of what happened could have been eliminated or at least minimized. God has reasons for His strategy regarding relationships. It behooves us all to take them seriously and obey His leading whatever the cost. A brief examination of events in the Garden

---

[129] 2 Samuel 15:9.

[130] 2 Samuel 18:33.

of Eden also provides considerable insight into the Lord's desire for communication. Shortly after Adam's creation, God conversed with him. For instance, the Lord said, "From any tree of the garden you may eat freely; but from the tree of the knowledge of good and evil you shall not eat, for in the day that you eat from it you shall surely die."[131] Yet even after sin entered into the picture in Genesis 3, God continued to communicate. Scripture certainly indicates that interaction is essential for connection, and this is particularly true in significant relational situations.

When gender dysphoria emerges within a close friendship, family, or similar relationship, some may wish to cut ties, not unlike David's response to Absalom. Indeed, considerable differences and breaks occur even among transgenders. One, for instance, who chose not to transition into the sex not determined at conception, complained that others refused to accept those who do not transition as not truly transgender. This individual noted that to "live as a trans person without transitioning is to be told constantly that you don't belong, that either you're not really trans or that you're denying your true nature." This hurting person continued, "If you object, you're ignored for as long as possible, and then called divisive [and] disruptive."[132] Moreover, there is the gay man who has been married to another man for twenty-five years. Yet this person was also a cross-dresser; he noted, "[T]hen it hit me. I'm transgender. All my life I've been the wrong sex. Finally, everything made sense. It explains what I've been feeling." This man admitted that he was "attracted

---

[131] Genesis 2:16b–17.

[132] Angus "Andrea" Grieve-Smith, "My Catalog of Woes," Trans-Blog August 23, 2016.

to straight men. My husband is gay. He's attracted to homosexual men. I'm a heterosexual girl."[133]

From these and other insights, one can see that there is a broad spectrum and considerable disagreement within the transgender, transsexual, and gender dysphoria communities, so one must be careful not to create a monolith. A lack of successful communication has much to do with this divisiveness. Each individual who views themself as a member of a sexually non-conformist group must be provided the freedom not to equate with all others. However, the gender fluid community attempts to determine an individual's uniqueness chiefly by their sexuality, particularly as its self-appointed gurus define it.[134] Nevertheless, no person's identity is determined solely on the basis of their sexuality. Without question, one's gender is a component, but not a primary defining factor.

Effective communication requires all parties to assume responsibility to hold a cursory understanding of some vital information. They should at the very least know, for instance, the recipient's personality, their sieves, and the message to be sent. Furthermore, they are to be aware of their own personality, how they appear to others, their filters, their message and other related information. Each individual has a unique set of strainers. For example, a transgender may be particularly sensitive to a message on that topic because they are adamant in their perceptions. Perhaps they

---

[133] Helen Boyd Kramer, (En)Gender "Gay cross-dresser Ex/Gender," Helen Boyd Kramer's journal on gender and stuff, August 16, 2016; See also Lisa Salazar, *Transparently: Behind the Scenes of a Good Life, self-published,* 2011.

[134] Numerous blogs on sites such as https://www.feedspot.com/?ref=blog; https://transequality.org/blog, https://blog.ted.com/7-talks-on-the-transgender-experience illustrate the point.

might be defensive because of previous conversations or experiences. Moreover, they might be concerned about how another transgender will respond to them as noted previously on "Andrea's" blog.

On the other hand, an evangelical may have other screens that skew the message. For instance, something could be delivered in an emotionally charged environment that automatically raises its impact exponentially. When someone is highly elated or enraged, for example, that person does not have full control over their emotional state. Thus, anything that enters through sensory perception will be highly tainted; likewise, any statement or action that comes from that individual will be exaggerated. If the receiver opposes the message content, its perception is often inflated. Hence, each conversant must watch for strainers because they can prompt the receiver or sender to hear or perceive a message that does not resemble what the remitter intended. Also remember that those who give the message have their own set of screens that can also have a profound effect on the communication. Unfortunately, unless a sender is keenly aware of their own filters as well as those of the recipient, little, if any regard is given to the respective sieves through which the message passes. After all, they are not readily apparent, yet they do play a vital role in relationships.[135]

Knowing ourselves is, in large part, being aware of our own sieves. A brief list includes, but is not limited to: How do we come across? Are we intimidating? What is our voice intonation? What type of language do we utilize? At what speed or volume do we speak? What non-verbal clues and gestures complement our verbal communication? How has the recipient interpreted messages in the past? Most people probably assign

---

[135] Barry L., *Effective Human Relations*, pp. 23–34.

little credence to such issues because they are typically unaware of their existence, but in order to maintain personal contact, they become crucial. We may perceive ourselves in a particular manner, but others might have a different perspective. By the same token, a person who takes offense at most anything that could possibly be construed as critical, needs to examine why. Hence, knowing oneself is an integral component of relating with each other. This is true for everyone, the transsexual, transgender, gender non-conforming, and the cisgender.[136]

Not only does one need to know their own deepest thoughts, hopes, dreams, attitudes, and similar mental attributes, but one also needs to be aware, at least to the degree possible, of the same for those with whom they are communicating. If, for instance, relations have been strained or are in any way unhealthy, all need to adjust the message to accommodate that unfortunate situation. Clearly, one cannot know that person to the degree that they do themselves, but all need to be as knowledgeable as they can. It is, of course, not possible to put oneself in another person's mental, emotional, psychological, and spiritual situation. But it is highly advisable to seek the Lord's direction, ask for His wisdom regarding what and how to relay a message, as well as what to communicate. Indeed, Holy Writ states "but if any of you lacks wisdom, let him ask of God, who gives to all men generously and without reproach, and it will be given to him."[137] God's omniscience includes the truth that He knows everything about us, including our thoughts, motives, attitudes, and objectives. By placing Him in control of our communication, both sending and receiving, we

---

[136] Reece, *Effective Human Relations*, pp. 35–42.

[137] James 1:5.

144

will minimize misunderstandings and misinterpretations. After all, that should be a primary objective.

Yet another consideration is the type of communication. It may be simpler to send an electronic mail, but this does not allow the sender to receive any immediate feedback that provides a clue regarding how the message was received. A telephone call will at least allow a hint of the response through vocal clues that can prompt the sender to tweak his or her delivery. A cursive letter will not allow for immediate feedback, but it does indicate to the recipient that the author believed the message was worth the extra effort of writing the correspondence as well as the expense of time, paper, envelope, and stamp.

When communicating with the individual(s) with whom one may have issues, it is essential to undergo an honest self-analysis, not unlike what the apostle Paul described in his initial letter to the Corinthians. Paul reported that many, if not most, in the Church made a mockery of communion, so he told the readers to examine themselves prior to partaking in the ordinance. If sin is present, confess, repent, and forsake it; or if someone has something against you, it is to be rectified. The Bible warns that anyone who "eats the bread or drinks the cup of the Lord in an unworthy manner shall be guilty of the body and of the blood of the Lord."[138] In one's self- examination, ask, "What precisely is my motive? Is it to pressure someone to change? Is it to shame the individual? Is it to condemn or promote guilt? If even a hint of those attitudes exists, it is time to take inventory of motives, desires, attitudes, and values. Are they biblical? Do they reflect the Spirit of Christ? Remember that the goal is to maintain a line of communication; ulterior motives and unhealthy attitudes make

---

[138] 1 Corinthians 11:27.

that objective nearly impossible to achieve. Indeed, Scripture indicates in Proverbs 18:19: "A brother offended is harder to be won than a strong city, and contentions are like the bars of a citadel." If the recipient perceives a message of condemnation, disapproval, or rejection, it is highly unlikely that interaction will continue unhindered.

In the parable of the prodigal son, the younger man returns home to his family. But for many, their loved one, acquaintance, friend, family member, or others, however, remain in the far country, alone, starving, and feeding the swine. How are they supposed to cope? Several suggestions deserve consideration. The first is to follow the example set by the father. Pray for the one whom they so desperately want to return to the Lord. "Draw near with confidence to the throne of grace...to receive mercy and...find grace to help in time of need."[139] Continue to turn that individual over to the Lord each day. He knows how to work effectively in their heart and His desire is for what is best to occur. Therefore, one is wise to let God have His way and ask that His Will be accomplished in their life. Another suggestion is to seek the Lord for wisdom regarding the truths He wants all to learn and for everyone involved to have the wisdom to apply those lessons in their own lives. Thirdly, one must ask the Holy Spirit to reveal any sin in his or her own heart and life and to provide no rest or peace until they confess, repent, and forsake their sin. If rebellion resides in one's own heart, how can that individual possibly expect God to prod another to surrender their disobedience? Yet a fourth suggestion is to ask the Father to open one's spiritual hearts, minds, and eyes to anything that they might be doing that hinders the loved one's return. Perhaps a particular personality trait, some mannerism, the perception

---

[139] Hebrews 4:16.

that one may unconsciously portray, the way that one comes across, or other deterrent may be obstructing the desired outcome. Place oneself completely in God's hands to allow Him, His Word, and the Holy Spirit to work in one's life, to make them someone to whom their loved one wants to return. Finally, if one has established a line of communication, maintain it. Keep it functioning, even if there is no response, the effort made will not go unnoticed. The loved one may or may not acknowledge it, but one may rest assured that the Father is completely aware. He may utilize the faithfulness in ways that one cannot even imagine. Therefore, if the circumstances seem to remain unabated, it is in everyone's best interest to allow the Lord to use the situation for His glory and everyone's edification. In the final analysis, an individual's obedience to Him will always produce the best result possible. It may be some time before one may see it come to fruition, but according to God's Word, it will arrive.

When discussing the issue of communication, by far the most important consideration is one's contact with the Lord. He desires for His own to spend time with Him. Indeed, humans were created for relationship with God. Often when individuals think about communication with the Father, their focus is on talking, including such things as praising Him or asking something of Him. This is essential; indeed, the Bible indicates in Hebrews 10:19–22, "Therefore brethren since we have confidence to enter the holy place by the blood of Jesus, by a new and living way which He inaugurated for us through the veil, that is, His flesh, and since we have a great priest over the house of God, let us draw near with a sincere heart in full assurance of faith...." But how much time do saints actually spend attentively listening to Him? When people think of communication, typically little if any time is consumed actively listening.

The Father, the Lord Jesus, and the Holy Spirit all have much to relate to humanity. Take for example the words of Christ as recorded in John 14:10: "Do you not believe that I am in the Father, and the Father is in Me? The words that I say to you I do not speak on my own initiative, but the Father abiding in Me does His works." The Son listened actively to the Father to receive His instructions as well as the words that He was to speak. Believers are to do the same. This same principle is described in John 16:13 where the Lord Jesus relates, "But when He, the Spirit of truth, comes, He will guide you into all the truth; for He will not speak on His own initiative, but whatever He hears, He will speak; and He will disclose to you what is to come." Just as the Son heard truth and instruction from the Father, so the Spirit receives from the Son what He is to disclose to humanity. Both the Son and the Spirit listened actively and intently to obtain the message to be proclaimed. The Father, the Son, and the Holy Spirit desire to do the same for people today. Indeed, the reason the Father provided the words was for the benefit of all. Not that God speaks in an audible voice, but rather to one's spirit. When people harbor issues such as hidden agendas, filters, apprehensiveness, and un-Christlike attitudes, the Lord's message becomes polluted. How foolish of humanity not to listen!

God is the source of wisdom. He is the one who will supply the essential information we need regarding communication with loved ones, friends, and others involved with transgender identity, transsexual identity, gender dysphoria, or any non-binary sexual expression. Indeed, He is the one who will open the spiritual heart, mind, and eyes to His truth. He will reveal the intentions of the heart. As Jeremiah 33:3 states, "Call to Me, and I will answer you, and I will tell you great and mighty things, which you do not know."

When considering the aspect of communication, assess one's own individual objective. Is it to facilitate one's personal but non-biblical self-righteousness? Is it being pursued with one's own strength to accomplish something that only God can do? What are the essential motives? What consideration has been given to the Father's desire? What role is played by various filters and other means of disrupting the message? Has any consideration been given to its feasibility or even safety for everyone involved? Communication is essential to any relationship; therefore, maintain the most important one. An individual's own personal relationship with the Father must be free of sin and open to fulfilling all of the Lord's commands. Remember Psalm 66:18–19: "If I regard wickedness in my heart, the Lord will not hear; but certainly God has heard; He has given heed to the voice of my prayer." Listen actively for his direction and obey immediately whatever He instructs. Being submissive to the Father is the key and it will always result in blessing, if for no other reason than to know that one is obedient to the Father.

CHAPTER 8

LESSONS FROM THE LORD

Then a shoot will spring from the stem of Jesse, and a branch
from his roots will bear fruit. And the Spirit of the Lord will rest
on Him, the spirit of wisdom and understanding, the spirit of
counsel and strength, the spirit of knowledge and the fear of
the Lord.

ISAIAH 11:1–2

God's Word instructs that once a person trusts Christ as personal
Lord and Savior, he or she is to be internally molded to the image
of Jesus. In Romans 8:29, for instance, the apostle Paul penned, "For those
whom He foreknew He also predestined to become conformed to the
image of His Son...." Later in that correspondence, Paul noted, "Do not
be conformed to this world but be transformed by the renewing of your
mind so that you may prove what the will of God is, that which is good

and acceptable and perfect."[140] The Greek term translated transformed, *metamorphoo,* is the same word rendered transfigured in Matthew 17:2. When Paul incorporates the word transformed, he is referring to a completely changed heart, mindset, worldview, thinking process, and thought pattern. He does not denote someone turning over a new leaf, stopping a bad habit, starting a good one, or initiating some improvement. He is describing one person becoming a completely different individual. Only the Lord can facilitate this change, but believers are to participate in the process called sanctification by reading and meditating on His Word, maintaining constant focus on him, and remaining in an attitude of prayer.

Peter noted in his first letter, chapter 1 verses 14–16: "As obedient children, do not be conformed to the former lusts which were yours in your ignorance, but like the Holy One who called you, be holy yourselves also in all your behavior; because it is written, 'You shall be holy for I am holy.'" A consistent theme throughout Holy Writ is that believers are to become more like Christ. In the Old Testament, one can locate a plethora of verses that reiterate this same principle. Psalm 119:9 reads, "How can a young man keep his way pure? By keeping it according to Your Word." Verse 11 proclaims, "Your Word have I treasured in my heart that I may not sin against You." Moses authored in Deuteronomy 23:14: "Since the Lord your God walks in the midst of your camp to deliver you and to defeat your enemies before you, therefore your camp must be holy; and He must not see anything indecent among you or He will turn away from you."

Scripture makes evident God's desire to teach truth and to reveal His

---

[140] Romans 12:2.

precepts to believers. Moreover, they are to absorb that knowledge, understanding, and wisdom to make personal application. By implementing that strategy, evangelicals will become more like the Son. How then does God unveil these truths? The opening verse in Hebrews provides insight into that intriguing question: "God, after He spoke long ago to the fathers in the prophets in many portions and in many ways, in these last days has spoken to us in His Son, whom He appointed heir of all things, through whom also He made the world." Cursory examinations of several Old Testament passages clearly illustrate God teaching His servants. In Judges 13:8, Manoah (Judge Samson's father) requested, "O Lord please let the man of God whom You have sent, come again to us that he may teach us what to do for the boy who is to be born." David wrote in Psalm 25:4–5, "Make me know Your ways O Lord; teach me Your paths. Lead me in Your truth and teach me, for You are the God of my salvation; for You I want all the day." On a more somber note regarding the Hebrews' attitude toward God, Jeremiah penned in 32:33: "They have turned their back to Me and not their face, though I taught them, teaching again and again they would not listen and receive instruction." The Lord instructs believers in part so they will learn to trust and to become like Him. The Holy Spirit who indwells Christians leads His sheep into all truth.

As part of being conformed to the image of Christ, the sovereign Lord allows situations, circumstances, and events to enter and influence His children's lives. Nothing occurs by accident but for a specific purpose. However, with finite human minds, that reason may not be understood. God permits believers to experience heartache, pain, grief, and troubles even to the point of despair. For instance, Paul relayed in 2 Corinthians 1:8, "For we do not want you to be unaware, brethren, of our affliction which came to us in Asia, that we were burdened excessively, beyond our strength, so that we despaired even of life...." The apostle continued, "Indeed we had the sentence of death within ourselves so that we would not trust in ourselves, but in God who raises the dead...." He further honored the Lord with his words, "who delivered us from so great a peril as death and will deliver us, He on whom we have set our hope." The life-threatening situation to which Paul alluded is undoubtedly an experience that he would not care to repeat. Nevertheless, the incident(s) further cemented in his heart and mind that whatever he encountered, the Father initiated for His glory and for the apostle's edification. The Lord often utilizes emotionally challenging familial and other relational experiences to teach His children important truths. If Christians allow them, any and all of their personal associations can reveal much about themselves. Furthermore, the myriad and often unanticipated situations that these relationships frequently prompt can illustrate the importance that a person places on their walk with God. Evangelicals who live in obedience to Him or may even be in the Lord's work are not immune to relational difficulties. The wicked one often sees these Christians as prime targets for attack. However, God allows those challenges for their benefit, to stimulate them to trust Him alone. .

For the Lord to use His servants most effectively, they must be completely broken. Believers whose lives reap the greatest harvest for the Lord are those who get to the point where they live the "life of grace," or as some may put it, the "crucified life." God gave to humanity a free will either to obey or disobey Him. Adam and Eve chose the latter, and since their action, all humans tend to rebel against the Father and seek independence. People are often taught self-reliance by incorporating available resources to accomplish whatever task they face. Individuals described as "self-made" are regularly cited as role models. The world frequently elevates them as individuals to emulate. In many respects, it is a helpful attitude that can be an effective tool for achieving lofty objectives, but not without God. One's personal walk with the Lord is the top priority and must always come first, before anyone or anything else. No one ever gets ahead in life or reaps eternal benefits by disobeying the Father. In his gospel, the apostle John explained this truth with an illustration of a fruit vine. The first two verses of chapter 15 read, "I am the true vine and My Father is the vinedresser. Every branch in me that does not bear fruit, He takes away; and every branch that bears fruit, He prunes so that it may bear more fruit." He continued in verses 4–5: "Abide in me, and I in you. As the branch cannot bear fruit of itself unless it abides in the vine, so neither can you unless you abide in me. I am the vine; you are the branches; he who abides in Me and I in him, he bears much fruit, for apart from Me you can do nothing."

In this passage, God's Word mentions at least two crucial principles with which every believer should be familiar. The first concerns personal salvation. If a person confesses to the Savior their own individual sinfulness and accepts the atoning crucifixion and resurrection of the Lord Jesus as the only and all sufficient payment for their personal sin, that individual receives everlasting life. It has nothing to do with joining a church or being baptized or participating in any other activity. No ritual will bring one to Christ. Rather, it reflects an individual relationship with the Father through the Son by the power of the Spirit.

After a person accepts the Lord Jesus as their personal Savior and trusts their eternal destiny to the Father through the Person of Jesus, they still need to be completely humbled, which leads to the second concept. Becoming a Christian involves far more than knowing the One from whom believers will never be separated. The Father wants the lives of His own to reflect His indwelling Spirit and to honor Him. That is how God provides what is best for believers. A life that honors the Savior is infinitely more fulfilling than one focused on self. Generally, the most effective means by which that occurs is through being completely humbled or broken. Only He knows how best to accomplish that task in a specific individual's life. For instance, it can be through any number of events, such as, but not limited to, a personal or family tragedy, serious illness, financial disaster, occupational catastrophe, or relational crisis through which the Lord removes one's ability to direct their personal circumstances.[141]

If one controls their surroundings, they are not broken. If, say, one always has enough money, they will never truly relate to what it means to go without. They do not understand what one experiences when they must depend on God to meet their needs. They will not comprehend brokenness in a financial sense. If someone experiences consistent intense pain for which there is no remedy, they must learn to depend upon God's grace. Someone in that situation can understand physical brokenness. Perhaps Paul explained it best in 2 Corinthians 12:7–9 where he wrote, "Because of the surpassing greatness of the revelations, for this reason, to keep me from exalting myself, there was given me a thorn in the flesh, a messenger of Satan to torment me—to keep me from exalting myself." He continued, "Concerning this I implored the Lord three times that it might

---

[141] Note that although the Lord may not cause these situations, He allows them. He uses them to facilitate one's humility or brokenness.

leave me. And He has said to me, 'My grace is sufficient for you, for power is perfected in weakness.'" The apostle concluded, "Most gladly, therefore, I will rather boast about my weaknesses, so that the power of Christ may dwell in me."

Another brief glimpse at the Greek might prove helpful to bring this into context. When most people consider the word "thorn," they might picture something like a floribunda rose, thistle, cactus, holly, honey locust tree, or some other type of thorn bush. The word translated thorn is *skolops*, which refers to a stake used for torture or impaling![142] In this context, it probably means that he had a physical disability that hindered his self-reliance. The point Paul makes is that God related to him, albeit painfully, that His grace is sufficient and that He was the apostle's provider. Paul was to operate under the power and influence of the Holy Spirit, to live by grace. Only when one surrenders their self-sufficiency does brokenness occur. Because individuals so reluctantly and hesitatingly cede that authority, many believers never experience biblical brokenness. Few actually grasp what it truly entails to live by grace alone, to comprehend that one exists only by His mercy, to live "the "crucified life" or the "life of grace." The Father is fully cognizant of what it will take to bring His children to the point of brokenness and to keep them completely surrendered to Him. It is, perhaps, ironic that only by being broken can believers ever become the men and women whom the Father intends for them to be. It is perhaps the only method by which believers can ever receive God's very best. Brokenness is the means that the Lord often uses to make a

---

[142] Charles Stanley, *The Life Principles Bible*, p. 1364.

person's life count for eternity.[143] Perhaps relational, familial, or other close association with transgender identity, transsexual identity or gender non-conformity is one's "thorn in the flesh." Maybe it is the means the Lord is using to break or humble you. If so, do not rebel against the Father but allow Him to do His transforming work. The life of Job is perhaps the quintessential example of how the Father allowed Satan to challenge a man with excruciating emotional agony, financial loss, and physically tortuous trials in the process of breaking someone. Satan brought on the circumstances, but the Father used them to transform Job into a stronger testimony for the Lord. Indeed, Job 23:10 reads, "But He knows the way I take; when He has tried me, I shall come forth as gold." Thousands of years following his physical death, Job's life continues to be a shining example to the mighty influence of a broken and surrendered man.

Satan continues to use all types of dastardly deeds to, in his depraved mind, harass, dishearten, and disappoint believers, turning them away from the Lord and destroying their witness for Christ. It is becoming more common for him to incorporate sexual non-conformity to distract believers and others from God's plan. When such deviance appears in any form, people will often become highly judgmental. Because sexual sins are committed against one's own body according to 1 Corinthians 6:18, many find them more heinous than other types of rebellion against the Lord. Furthermore, American society tends to categorize sexual sins by implying that some are worse than others. For example, believers often perceive that adultery or fornication is a less serious sin than, say, homosexuality, transsexual identity, or transgender identity. The reason

---

[143] See, for instance, Charles Stanley, *The Blessings of Brokenness: Why God Allows Us to Go Through Hard Times,* (Grand Rapids: Zondervan, 1997).

perhaps is because society is more willing to accept sin of a heterosexual nature than that which is not. Indeed, terms are often coined to make those sins appear more acceptable. For instance, words or phrases such as "an affair" "premarital or extramarital sex" sound much more palatable than "adultery," "fornication," or "sodomy." The apostle John assimilated in his gospel perhaps the quintessential example of dealing with sexual sin by his description in 8:7b of the incident when the Scribes and Pharisees brought a woman caught in the act of adultery and asked Jesus what to do. He wisely answered, "He who is without sin among you let him be the first to throw a stone at her." Jesus knew the religious leaders were guilty of much wickedness even if it was not of a sexual nature. Many undoubtedly fostered "secret sins" or those which the individual foolishly thought were unknown to all. They seemed oblivious to the passage recorded in Numbers 32:20–23 where Moses issued a series of commands, and warned, "But if you will not do so, behold, you have sinned against the Lord, and be sure your sin will find you out." Hence, they could not convict her until they confessed, repented, and forsook their own rebellion. Indeed, the clear biblical admonition is that believers are not to condemn. Matthew 7:1 reads, "Do not judge so that you will not be judged. For in the way you judge, you will be judged; and by your standard of measure, it will be measured to you." That does not mean believers approve and accept sin, but what it does indicate is that all are sinful beings and are fully responsible for their own actions. The apostle Matthew and the doctor Luke incorporated into their gospels the account of one who was quick to condemn sin in another while he himself was replete with debauchery. Jesus described that individual as a charlatan by saying in Matthew 6:42b,

"You hypocrite, first take the log out of your own eye, and then you will see clearly to take the speck out of your brother's eye."

Unmistakably, the fact of the matter is that sin is sin. Its consequences are severe, its final result is death; for the unbeliever, eternal separation from the Father, both spiritual and physical. When someone's friend, family member, prayer partner, or other close individual, especially one who has put their faith and trust in Jesus as their personal Savior, deviates from God's path, it should prompt grief in at least two ways. Firstly, it decreases the wayward family member's or close friend's sensitivity to the Holy Spirit and His convicting work in their own life, making them more susceptible to Satan's deceit. Those who remain faithful to the Lord must visualize themselves among the Scribes and the Pharisees who wanted to stone the adulterous woman. When that occurs, believers who take seriously their walk with the Lord can see their foolish attempt, with a plank in their own eye, to remove another's speck. When such thoughts cross one's mind, it is indeed extremely beneficial for them to thank the Holy Spirit for His convicting power. In his confession recorded in Psalm 51, a repentant David acknowledged, "For I know my transgressions, and my sin is ever before me." He continued to plead, "Create in me a clean heart O God, and renew a steadfast spirit within me." Also noted in his admission, "The sacrifices of God are a broken spirit; a broken and a contrite heart, O God, you will not despise."[144] David's confession occurred several months following his adultery with Bathsheba and his murder of Uriah. He had become arrogant and haughty which hindered his sensitivity to sin. When Nathan reprimanded the King for his behavior, he immediately confessed, repented, and forsook his rebellion against the Father. He

---

[144] Psalm 51:3, 10, 17.

did not blame others, society, culture, his upbringing, family, or make any excuses. David placed himself completely at God's mercy. When believers become aware of others' sins, they must never become conceited or arrogant like the Scribes, the Pharisees, Sadducees, and the hypocrites did toward the adulterous woman. Rather, their responsibility is to open themselves completely to the Holy Spirit. Allow Him to bring to their attention their own sin, rebellion, pride, and disobedience. Paul related in his first correspondence to Timothy that he (Paul) was the worst sinner, in part because of his earlier work killing and imprisoning believers and attempting to destroy the Church. Hence, evangelicals, too, like Paul, must take constant inventory of their own lives, and respond immediately to the Spirit's leading and direction.

This leads to the second source of grief, which occurs when one who lives by grace perceives how that person's actions stand in the way of God's best for their life. A believer wants what is best for themselves as well as other believers. A Christian grieves when another rebels against the Lord. Indeed, in Mark 3:5 a man with a withered hand came to Jesus. Several religious leaders thought it inappropriate for the Lord to heal him on the Sabbath. "After looking at them with anger, grieved at their hardness of heart, He said to the man, 'Stretch out your hand.' And he stretched it out, and his hand was restored." The unbelief and rebellion of the Pharisees, Scribes, and Sadducees brought grief to the Lord. He understood that by their actions they rejected Him and His plan for them. The same attitude should arise in an evangelical when another turns away from the Lord. If a friend, acquaintance, family member, or close associate rejects the Father's plan for sexuality and chooses a non-conforming path, the grief becomes intense. Yet when that person realizes their sin and returns to the Lord, a spirit of rejoicing occurs, much as did the father when his prodigal son returned.

The Father has a two-part plan for each individual. Initially, He desires that all should come to repentance. For example, in his second epistle, Peter explained in 3:9 that "the Lord is not slow in His promises...but is...not wishing that any should perish but for all to come to repentance." In his initial correspondence to Timothy, Paul penned in 2:3-4, "This is good and acceptable in the sight of God our Savior, who desires all men to be saved and to come to the knowledge of the truth." Once an individual obeys the Lord's first part of His plan for their life, they begin the second, through which they are conformed to the image of the Lord Jesus. His desire encompasses a believer's entire being; their essence, identity, mind, soul, and spirit are to become thoroughly intertwined with Him. They are to reach the point of living the "life of grace" or the "crucified life."

Those who choose an atypical sexual expression are searching in part for their personal distinctiveness not in Christ but in a satanic substitute. Preadolescents tend to find their identity with their family of origin, but as they age and mature their self-perceptions normally change as well. For example, during the teenage years, it often becomes more closely aligned with non-familial elements. Personal achievements, interests, desires, and goals become more significant. Later in life, a career, financial status, education, and family of procreation become predominant. However, none of these reflect God's design in that they do not reflect a believer's identity in Him. During the past few decades, some have transferred their individuality chiefly to sexual abnormalities along with an agenda promoting their behavioral pursuits. Indeed, they have adopted a peculiar term, coined by George Weinberg in the 1960s—homophobia, against or fear of the same—to describe those who disagree with their conduct or beliefs. If one's choice of sexual expression becomes the source of their identity, they clearly miss the Father's purpose for their life. It becomes completely self-focused rather than God-centered. From an eternal perspective, it is far better to allow the Lord to live His life in and through His Spirit who indwells and empowers all believers. One may easily counter with the statement, "It is my life and I can do as I please." That, however, is inaccurate. Granted, a person can, to some degree, do as they please, but it is not their life because, as Paul so succinctly explained in his first letter to the Church at Corinth, 6:20: "For you have been bought with a price: therefore glorify God in your body." The apostle Peter warned in his second letter 2:1 that false teachers "will secretly introduce destructive heresies, even denying the sovereign Lord who bought them—bringing swift destruction on themselves."

In all the information that refers to a transgender, transsexual, or gender variant, little, if any, describes a broken individual who unashamedly espouses for Christ, lives completely devoted to Him, reads and meditates on Scripture daily, and is sensitive to the Holy Spirit's leading. Yet virtually all the materials prepared by gender non-conformists demonstrates a low view of the Bible, a non-scriptural concept of God, and a dim view of evangelicals and those who live a "crucified life" or a "life of grace." They are not infrequently described with derogatory terms. Yet by doing so they become guilty of the very charges with which they often condemn believers. For many of those with friends, loved ones, and others involved with such lifestyles, grief becomes a constant companion.

If one accepts the sovereignty of God along with the two primary goals He has for believers (their personal salvation, and their becoming conformed to Jesus' image, or sanctification), they are then forced by simple logic to acknowledge that He allows transgender identity, transsexual identity, gender dysphoria, or gender non-conformity to enter into their family, circle of friends, or relationships for a specific purpose. The Father knows how each person functions. He is fully cognizant of one's intellect, emotional makeup, and will; in fact, He knows individuals better than they do themselves. He permits believers to experience what seems like an insurmountable burden so they will see it is far beyond anything they can deal with on their own. Satan, however, in his scheme to disrupt the Father's will, tempts believers to travel down that exhausting and spiritually draining trek of dealing with the situation alone. His warped strategy is to cause significant if not irreparable damage to one's spiritual, mental, emotional, and/or physical health.

Still, however, there are those who refuse to follow the Lord's command to "humble yourselves, therefore, under the mighty hand of God, that He may exalt you at the proper time, casting all your anxiety upon Him, because He cares for you."[145] Moreover, Matthew 11:28–30 describes what Jesus wants believers to do with their intense emotional and spiritual burden: "Come to Me, all who are weary and heavy-laden, and I will give you rest. Take My yoke upon you and learn from Me, for I am gentle and humble in heart, and you will find rest for your souls. For My yoke is easy and My burden is light." Doing this, however, is most certainly easier said than done since humans naturally want to take care of things themselves. Even Christians often believe that they have the best solution, that they can handle whatever comes their way. However, by operating under that premise, they tend to rely on their own strength which is soon depleted

---

[145] 1 Peter 5:6–7.

and leads to anger, a sense of loss, frustration, loss of control, or bewilderment. Fortuitously, as individuals fail to handle the situation under their own strength, knowledge, and wisdom, some will finally begin to comprehend exactly what God wants believers to realize; that they are powerless. When they get to that point, and only while in that condition, will they give their problems to Him. The Father never intended for believers to experience life on their own carrying burdens that drag them down. His ultimate desire is for His children to give Him those grievous experiences and weighty encumbrances be they intellectual, emotional, relational, spiritual, financial, or any other problematic circumstance.

Thus, if believers allow Him, the Father will take them to the place where they can honestly and truthfully ask the Lord, "What do you want me to learn from this? What are you showing or revealing to me? How can this situation make me more like You and more clearly reflect Your indwelling Holy Spirit?" It is also helpful to request that the Father glorify Himself as He works in and through the situation. Once a person arrives at that point, the burden of blaming himself or herself for the situation is lifted and the Holy Spirit takes control. "But when He, the Spirit of truth, comes, He will guide you into all the truth; for He will not speak on His own initiative, but whatever He hears, He will speak; and He will disclose to you what is to come. He will glorify Me, for He will take of Mine and will disclose it to you."[146] The prodigal son had to reach the bottom—a Jewish man living amongst and feeding swine—before he "came to himself." Likewise, believers must reach that same point before they will truly begin to fathom the truth God wants them to grasp and inculcate into their lives. He will work in anyone's life to demonstrate His mercies that

---

[146] John 16:13–14.

are new every morning, touch them with His grace by which He sustains them moment by moment, and express His faithfulness beyond measure. Finally, He maintains His eternal promise never to leave His children or forsake them.

Jesus is the vine, saints are the branches. Believers are called to allow the Lord to work in and through them to produce the fruit of the spirit which is then manifested by the branches. When someone sees a believer's life beneath the façade, what precisely do they encounter? The world is watching in so many ways. Believers do the same. What or who do they see? Someone whose identity is extrinsically dependent upon the temporal, or one who has their intrinsically predicated identity based upon their position in Christ? Will they view an individual who allows the Holy Spirit, His Word, and the Lord Jesus to mold them into God's image, or one who refuses to let the Lord work in their life? Do they see the fruit of the spirit as listed in Galatians 5:22–23 or are they met by the fruit of the flesh as noted in 5:19–21? Paul referred chiefly to his finances when he wrote Philippians 4:11, "Not that I speak from want, for I have learned to be content in whatever circumstances I am." Nevertheless, those words may be applied to any set of conditions. Indeed, for the benefit and spiritual growth of Christians, to bring them to the place where their ultimate desire is for God's will to be fulfilled, even if it means heartache, pain, emotional distress, or even physical agony. Jesus permits them to experience a miniscule microcosm of what He sensed in the garden of Gethsemane when He prayed in Luke 22:42: "Father, if You are willing, remove this cup from Me; yet not My will, but Yours be done." Likewise, while on the cross when He exclaimed in Matthew 27:46b, "*Eli, Eli, lama sabachthani?*" that is, "'My God, My God, why has Thou forsaken me?'"

A perceptive believer whom the Lord is taking through a deep, dark, depressive, and desolate valley will seek to learn lessons from the Lord. Perhaps the primary truth is that He is instructing them to trust in Him, obey Him, and experience His peace. Think, for example, of Joseph. He was sold into slavery by his brothers and became the servant to Potipher. The Egyptian's wife falsely accused Joseph of attempted rape which prompted his placement in the Pharaoh's prison. He spent many years in those despairing conditions yet Scripture does not mention that he expressed any negative words or attitudes. In God's time, Joseph was released from incarceration and elevated to Prime Minister. The Lord may be utilizing this time to prepare a saint whom He will use in mighty ways to further the Kingdom. Allow the Father to use relational or familial sexual non-conformity or whatever circumstance to mold you into the woman or man He has called you to be. In his first epistle, Peter addressed Christians who were being persecuted for their beliefs. The truth he expressed in 5:6–7 is just as applicable today as it was nearly 2,000 years ago. "Humble yourselves therefore, under the mighty hand of God, that He may exalt you at the proper time, casting all your anxiety upon Him, because He cares for you."

CHAPTER 9

EPILOGUE

Trust in the Lord with all your heart, and do not lean on your own understanding. In all your ways acknowledge Him, and He will make your paths straight. Do not be wise in your own eyes; fear the Lord and turn away from evil. It will be healing to your body, and refreshment to your bones.

PROVERBS 3:5–8

After reading this monograph, one may wonder what steps to take regarding relational or familial transgender identity, transsexual identity, non-binary sexual expression, or other forms of gender non-conformity. What then may one glean from this brief examination? How does someone apply the information to their own personal difficulties? Although this work is directed primarily toward sexual and gender non-conformity, others may face different challenges such as unbelief, drug/alcohol addiction, criminal behavior, abusive relationships, or a host of other un-Christlike behaviors. With whatever challenges one faces, the wicked one and his demons use essentially the same strategy and tactics with only minor alterations. First of all, he wants to make evangelicals feel isolated, like they are the only ones facing their particular relational issue. If he can separate believers from one another, they become much more vulnerable and susceptible to his cunning deceitfulness. As Ecclesiastes 4:12 reminds readers, "If one can overpower him who is alone, two can resist him. A cord of three strands is not quickly torn apart." When individuals in similarly challenging situations remain united by focusing upon the Lord rather than the circumstances or themselves, they become considerably stronger and make the situation more difficult for Satan.

Secondly, expressing one's emotions to others may provide some amelioration. This strategy can be exercised in various ways. For example, speaking with trusted confidants, especially those who have traversed or are in the midst of similar valley experiences, can provide empathy available from no other human source. One may, perhaps, find it helpful to express their emotions on paper. Writing one's thoughts is often beneficial in several ways. For instance, it generally minimizes rumination. Constantly rehearsing one's errors, whether real or imagined, or repeating how one has been done wrong is not helpful. Lucifer, however, loves to utilize this self-deprecating behavior to demoralize believers. But once an individual places his or her feelings and ideas on paper, Satan loses a major weapon in his arsenal. That person has positioned those problematic ideas in an observable and discernable location. When someone can peruse their thoughts, it helps put everything into perspective. One's patterns of contemplation begin to emerge and demonstrate how they are or are not helpful. Visualizing one's thoughts and reading their thinking patterns can reveal previously unknown or hidden personal characteristics such as selfishness, poor attitudes, self-righteousness, arrogance, or perhaps spiritual immaturity. Utilizing newly discovered insight can revitalize a person's thoughts and emotions. Finally, the Holy Spirit can use someone's own words to bring them to terms with their situation. The Father opened the prodigal son's heart and mind so he understood his wrong thinking. God revealed to King David his heinous sin regarding Uriah and Bathsheba as the monarch recorded in Psalm 51 and elsewhere. He can and will do the same for anyone wise enough to allow Him to do so.

A third suggestion is not to view the situation with an either-or resolution. Do not succumb to the trap that God maintains degrees of sin. Much if not most of life is black and white with a clear line of demarcation. There is a right response to a situation as well as one or more corresponding erroneous reaction(s). Clearly, this is based on the concept of absolute truth. Sin, for example, is sin, and its consequence is death. Moreover, "If we say that we have no sin, we are deceiving ourselves and the truth is not in us. If we confess our sins, He is faithful and righteous to forgive us our sins and to cleanse us from all unrighteousness. If we say that we have not sinned, we make Him a liar and His word is not in us."[147] What many may not understand is that if their loved one is involved in certain types of wickedness, the ultimate earthly result can be more serious than the consequence of different sins. For example, sexual sins can result in serious infections, viruses, and diseases. Yet those involved in such are not more culpable than individuals who commit more socially and culturally acceptable iniquities such as pride, deceit, lying, harboring wrong attitudes, envy, or gossip.

---

[147] 1 John 1:8–10.

Although one may be grieved by relational or familial transgender identity, transsexual identity, homosexuality, non-binary sexual expression, or any other transgression, all may be absolved. By confessing one's sin and requesting His forgiveness, all wrongdoing is covered by the blood of Christ. However, for unbelief there is no provision of pardon. Only those who make a deliberate, willful, and cognitive choice to accept Jesus' atoning death on the cross alone to pay their sin debt will receive the forgiveness He so freely offers. There is absolutely nothing any person can do to make themselves acceptable to God, to pay the penalty for sin. Hence, it is only through the Father's mercy and grace that believers will spend eternity with Him. Rebellion toward God by anyone with whom one has a relationship, such as a friend, acquaintance, or family member pierces to the depths of a believer's very being. Indeed, an evangelical's great yearning should be that all invest their life for eternity. Nevertheless, that person living in disobedience to God is not beyond the mercy, grace, and *agape* of the Father. As Hebrews 4:16 instructs, continue taking that individual and oneself "with confidence to the throne of grace, that we may receive mercy and may find grace to help in time of need."

Yet another recommendation from these chapters is not to become enslaved to the wisdom of this world. That understanding is not from God and leads its followers down a dark path that results in destruction. Recall Proverbs 16:25, "There is a way which seems right to a man, but its end is the way of death." For instance, reject the erroneous notion that believers simply must accept everyone as they are. Acceptance may be a means of minimizing arguments and easing tensions, at least temporarily, but it is not a method to promote a close, personal, intimate, and growing relationship with the Lord Jesus. Refusal to assent does not mean that evangelicals are to condemn. Indeed, during his conversation with Nicodemus, Jesus said in John 3:17, "For God did not send the Son into the world to judge the world, but that the world might be saved through Him." Rather, it requires that saints lovingly share the message of salvation through the sacrificial blood of the Lamb of God. He offers true, complete, total, and permanent freedom and peace. By accepting His atoning death, the door is opened to the euphoria that only a relationship with Christ can offer. It is a much greater option than accepting the world's dysphoria.

Another item to absorb is the fact that much of the ostensibly scientific data purported by mainstream media is highly misleading, even erroneous. Many so-called scientists provide unsupported arguments from hopelessly flawed studies to promote unfounded but culturally popular concepts such as a biological etiology of homosexuality and transgender identity, among other things. Whatever one may read, remember that there is no organic basis that causes or even prompts homosexuality, transgender identity, transsexual identity, gender dysphoria, non-binary sexual expression, or any combination thereof. Nevertheless, researchers will continue to rummage through previous studies; conduct biased, disingenuous, and deceptive inquiries; and publish allegedly new discoveries. Indeed, while in the final stages of preparing this manuscript two new studies emerged. One concentrated on the increased rate of homosexuality among younger sons in families with older brothers. But like the others on this subject, it refuses to examine the unexplored but highly probable influence of the relationship between the brothers and other familial ties. It is, in essence, a rehash of what is already available. Its author, Ray Blanchard, has not been forthcoming regarding his private life.[148] Indeed, a blogger noted, "Andrea James's article of November 2009 is by far the best on this particular topic, but I would maintain that [Blanchard's] closetry denies him the right to claim to be gay."[149]

A second project centered on yet another search for a gene causing gay behavior. Not surprisingly, the study proved unsuccessful. Furthermore, Benjamin Neale, one of its leading researchers, is homosexual with a sociocultural agenda. He couched the nebulous results with the tentative and unimpressive statements "We've clarified that there's a lot of diversity out there." Furthermore, "This moves our understanding (of same-sex sex) to a deeper and more nuanced place." Moreover, the study was closely analyzed by several non-binary sexually expressing individuals including Zeke Stokes, of the US-based LGBTQ rights group GLAAD, who concluded that it "re-confirms the long-established understanding that there is no conclusive degree to which nature or nurture influence how a gay or lesbian person behaves."[150] A more realistic if not accurate perception may be located at National Public Radio which announced that "A huge new study finds a faint hint of genetic variation that may be linked to same-sex behavior. The study broadly reinforces the observation that both biology and a person's environment influence sexuality, but the results reveal very little about that biology."[151]

Culture is fluid as we noted in the chapter on Philosophical,

---

[148] https://transgendermap.com/?s=Ray+Blanbchard.

[149] https://zagria.blogspot.com/2009/11/ray-blanchard-1945-psychologist.html.

[150] Melinda Mills, "Perspective Genomics: How do genes affect same-sex behavior?" *Science*, August 30, 2019, Vol. 365, Issue 6456, pp. 869–870.

[151] Richard Harris, "Search for 'Gay Genes' Comes up Short in Large New Study," All

Theological, and Historical Foundations of Transgender Identity. What at one time was considered outrageous and unthinkable becomes acceptable and encouraged. Remember that God's immutable Word does not change with the fickle winds of society and culture. Malachi 3:6 assures us, "For I the Lord do not change." One reads in Hebrews 13:8, "Jesus Christ is the same yesterday and today, yes and forever." Hence, the fact that the Father, the Son, and the Holy Spirit will never change is a truth in which we may place our complete and eternal confidence. Anything that contradicts Scripture is not of God. The world, however, is at war with believers. Note the words of the apostle Paul, "For though we walk in the flesh, we do not war according to the flesh, for the weapons of our warfare are not of the flesh, but divinely powerful for the destruction of fortresses." Paul's correspondence to the Corinthians continues, "We are destroying speculations and every lofty thing raised up against the knowledge of God and we are taking every thought captive to the obedience of Christ, and we are ready to punish all disobedience, whenever your obedience is complete."[152]

A primary battlefield in this constant conflict is the mind. Hence, it is crucial that every thought is individually analyzed. Is it congruent with God and His Word? If not, it is from Satan or one of his minions. He is the father of lies, so reject it immediately.[153] Contrariwise, take

---

Things Considered, August 29, 2019, National Public Radio, https://www.npr.org/sections/health-shots/2019/08/29/755484917/do-genes-play-a-role-in-who-you-have-sex-with-large-study-explores-a-tricky-ques.

[152] 2 Corinthians 10:3–6.

[153] John 8:44c.

the thoughts from the Lord and follow David's example as recorded in Psalm 143:5-6. "I remember the days of old; I meditate on all thy doings; I muse on the work of they hands. I stretch out my hands to Thee; my soul longs for Thee, as a parched land." Because of this continuous warfare, the indefatigable movers and shakers behind cultural and social change work tirelessly to discredit and destroy the Word. If God is removed, He no longer hinders human behavior. Eliminating absolute truth ushers in the deadly but prevalent trinity of cultural relativism, pragmatism, and pluralism.

Commonly expressed sociocultural wisdom states that if an individual struggles with an emotional loss or grief they will experience several stages until they come to acceptance. When that occurs the individual will sense a release from their internal bondage and be at peace with the situation. This, however, is incongruent with Scripture. Peace comes only from a relationship with Christ. Indeed, in the fifth chapter in his letter to the Galatians Paul notes that peace is a fruit of the Spirit. It is not an emotion nor is it something that comes by accepting a particular scenario. Rather it is produced within us by the Holy Spirit through our relationship to Him. Reject the conventional wisdom of acceptance regarding emotional or physical pain or grief and allow the Father to use it in your life to grow in the Lord and to be a vibrant testimony to others.

Yet another morsel to reap from the book is to reject the allure of self-pity or defeatism but glean from the Father what He is teaching you. As believers in God's sovereignty, and in the fact that following salvation evangelicals are to be transformed into the image of Christ, everything that enters into a Christian's life is designed for His glory and for one's personal spiritual growth and maturity. Granted, Satan can and will orchestrate some circumstances, but the omnipotent Father will use those events for the good of His own. Instead of complaining to God by asking why He permitted such a trial to enter one's life, ask Him specifically what He would have one learn. Difficult but essential lessons are absorbed from extremely painful circumstances. According to Matthew 11:29, the Son wants us to rely on Him: "Take My yoke upon you, and learn from Me, for I am gentle and humble in heart; and you shall find rest for your souls." When He teaches an important truth, He allows believers to experience situations that force them truly to internalize that lesson and to depend solely upon Him.

If at all possible, work diligently to maintain a line of communication with the transgender, transsexual, or gender variant. The Lord wants to facilitate a relationship with His own and He provided His Son to make that possible. Believing friends, family, and others with relationships involving the transgender or gender non-conforming individual should not normally terminate those relationships. The individual remains one's friend, acquaintance, associate, or family member. That relationship is based upon who that person is, not what that individual does. Granted, there are circumstances where communicating with one's friend, associate, or loved one may place at risk the individual's personal safety and/or well-being. If that is the case, or if the person has blocked any interaction, one cannot make it happen. The prodigal son relocated to a distant land perhaps in part to prevent any familial contact. Indeed, the Father probably did not know where his son lived. Even in the modern world, some situations arise that preclude any communication. But when the son allowed it by returning, the Father certainly resumed contact. No matter how difficult, believers will do well to maintain a similar attitude. Humans are social beings and relationships are paramount. Familial relationships and friendships are foundational and, when possible, maintaining them is essential.

By far the most important thing to glean from this work is to know for certain that everyone in your familial, church, and relational circle enjoys a close, personal, intimate, and growing relationship with the Father. Some may wonder how it is possible to know if one has that relationship, but Scripture is eminently clear on the subject. "These things I have written to you who believe in the name of the Son of God, so that you may know that you have eternal life."[154] This includes any transgender, gender variant, gender or sexual non-conformist, or non-binary sexually expressing individual. Remember that sin is sin, and no sin, except for unbelief, is beyond the cleansing power of Jesus' blood. If one's friend, associate, family member, transgender or cisgender has never admitted to the Lord the fact of one's own personal sinfulness and asked Him for forgiveness solely on the basis of Jesus' atoning death, please do so. It is unmistakably by far the greatest, most important, longest lasting, and most far-reaching decision anyone can ever make. Yet by rebuffing the Savior or refusing to make a choice, one rejects the opportunity and sets one on a course of eternal loss. But as long as one has the ability to select that option, God's offer stands.

If any in one's relationship circle made that decision but drifted from the Lord or refuses to let God do His transforming work, salvation is not lost, but the joy has departed.[155]

---

[154] 1 John 5:13.

[155] Recall, for example, King David's supplication in Psalm 51:12, "Restore to me the joy

Repent of sin and return to the one who died for all. Allow Him to take control of one's very being, spend time with Him in the Word, in prayer, meditate on Scripture, set one's mind on the Father and obey His instructions. Permit God to do His transforming work in the depths of one's very being as well as in the heart and mind of one's transgender, transsexual, gender non-conforming or non-binary sexually expressing friend, associate or loved one. See how He can mend the brokenhearted, clean the vilest sinner, forgive the most heinous sin, set the captive free, and provide the peace that passes understanding.

---

of your salvation and sustain me with a willing spirit."

EPILOGUE

We have examined a number of aspects regarding familial transgenderism. What then may we glean from this brief journey? How do we apply the information presented to our own personal difficulties? First of all, remember that this is only one issue with which our family struggles. Yours may have other challenges with offspring such as unbelief, fornication, adultery, homosexuality, drug/alcohol addiction, criminal behavior, abusive relationships or a host of other un-Christlike behaviors. With whatever problem(s) we face the wicked one and his demons use essentially the same strategy and tactics with only minor alterations. First of all he wants to make us feel alone, like we are the only ones facing this issue. If he can separate us from each other we become much more vulnerable and susceptible to his cunning deceitfulness. As Ecclesiastes 4:12 reminds us "if one can overpower him who is alone, two can resist him. A cord of three strands is not quickly torn apart." When parents and others in similar situations stick together with the Lord we become considerably stronger and make the situation more difficult for Satan.

Secondly, it can be helpful to express our emotions to others. Indeed, much of this book's original draft was essentially recollections of conversations with my parents. Talks with Mom and Dad in the early stages of our difficulties, which centered on homosexuality, were highly beneficial. Their parental experiences in bringing up five children provided a depth of knowledge and insight. They allowed and even counseled us to speak freely of our deep and intense pain, heartache, and grief. Nearly always they prayed with us, taking the situation to the Father Himself. Furthermore, they encouraged us to carry on, that we were doing well with the situation although we often felt like miserable failures. When Mom went to be with the Lord I used her Bible to prepare and deliver the Eulogy. In it was her prayer list and at the top was our child's name. During later conversations with Dad, after transgenderism entered the picture, his approach was similar. He permitted and urged us to converse and he continually offered his prayers and encouragement; telling us how well we were doing and that continuing that path was the wisest course. He too prayed for our family by name every morning following breakfast. What a comfort my parents were until they entered the Father's presence.

Along with the strategy of speaking with trusted confidants it is helpful to express your emotions on paper. Writing your thoughts is helpful in several ways. First of all, it will normally minimize rumination. Constantly rehearsing our errors, repeating how we have been done wrong is not helpful, but Lucifer loves to use it for our detriment. Once we place our feelings and ideas on paper Satan loses a major weapon in his arsenal. Secondly, when we can peruse our thoughts it helps put everything into perspective. Our patterns of contemplation begin to emerge and we can see how they are or are not helpful. Visualizing what we think and reading our perspectives can lead to our becoming apprised of unseen selfishness or perhaps spiritual maturity. Utilizing that fresh insight can revitalize our thoughts and emotions. Finally the Lord can use our own words to bring us to terms with the situation. Just as the Father opened the prodigal son's mind so he understood his wrong thinking. God revealed to King David his heinous sin regarding Uriah and Bathsheba as the Monarch recorded in Psalm 51 and elsewhere; He can and will do the same for us if we allow Him to do so.

A third suggestion is not to view this as an either/or situation. Much of life is black and white with a clear line of demarcation. Sin, for example, is sin, and its consequence is death. Yes, our children sin as do we. But what many do not understand is that if their child is involved in wickedness, its ultimate earthly result may be more serious than other sin such as pride, deceitfulness, lies, wrong attitudes or gossip of which we may well be guilty. Nevertheless, all have sinned and fall short of the glory of God, and the wages of sin is death. Although we as parents are grieved by familial transgenderism, transsexualism, homosexuality, or any other iniquity, all may be absolved. By confessing our sin and requesting His forgiveness all is covered by the blood of Christ. However, for unbelief there is no provision of pardon. Only those who make a deliberate, willful, and cognitive choice to accept Jesus' atoning death on the cross to pay their sin debt will receive the forgiveness He so freely offers. Hence it is only through The Father's mercy and grace that believers will spend eternity with Him. Although our family member's rebellion pierces to the depth of our very being, that person is not beyond the mercy, grace and *agape* of the Father. As Hebrews 4:16 instructs, continue taking that individual and ourselves "with confidence to the throne of grace, that we may receive mercy and may find grace to help time of need."

Yet another recommendation from these chapters is not to fall for what seems to be the wisdom of this world. It is not from God and will lead us down a dark path that leads to destruction. For instance, as discussed in the chapter on acceptance, reject the erroneous notion that we simply must accept everyone as they are. Acceptance may be a means of minimizing arguments but it is not a method to promote a close, personal, intimate and growing relationship with the Lord Jesus. That does not mean that we condemn, rather it requires that we lovingly share the message of salvation through the sacrificial blood of the Lamb of God. He offers true, complete, total, and permanent freedom and peace. By accepting His atoning death the door is opened to the euphoria that only a relationship with Christ can offer. It is a much greater option than accepting the world's dysphoria.

Culture is fluid as we noted in the chapter on philosophical developments. What at one time was considered outrageous and unthinkable becomes acceptable and encouraged. Many so called scientists provide unsupported arguments to promote unfounded but culturally popular concepts such as a biological cause to homosexuality and transgenderism among other things. Remember that God's immutable Word does not change with the fickle winds of society and culture. Malachi 3:6 assures us "For I the Lord do not change." We read in Hebrews 13:8 "Jesus Christ is the same yesterday and today, yes and forever." The fact that neither the Father, the Son, not the Holy Spirit ever change is a truth in which we may place our complete trust. Anything that contradicts Scripture is not of God. Therefore the powers behind culture and society do what they can to discredit and destroy the Word. If God is removed He no longer hinders human behavior. Eliminating absolute truth ushers in the deadly but prevalent philosophy of relativism.

Yet another morsel to reap from the book is to ask God what He is teaching you. As believers in God's sovereignty, and in the fact that following salvation we are to be transformed into the image of Christ, everything that enters into our life is designed for His glory and for our spiritual growth. Granted, Satan can and will orchestrate some circumstances, but our omnipotent Father will use those events for our good. Instead of complaining to God by asking why He permitted such a trial to enter our life, ask Him specifically what He would have you acquire. Difficult lessons are absorbed from extremely painful circumstances. According to Matthew 11:29 the Son wants us to rely on Him. "Take My yoke upon you, and learn from Me, for I am gentle and humble in heart; and you shall find rest for your souls." When He wants us to learn an important truth He allows us to experience situations that force us to depend solely upon Him.

If at all possible work diligently to maintain a line of communication. The Lord desires to facilitate a relationship with us and He provided His Son to make that possible. As parents we assumed responsibility to rear our child(ren) in the nurture and admonition of the Lord. Granted there are circumstances where communicating with our loved one may place at risk our personal safety and/or well-being. If that is the case or if the individual has blocked any interaction we cannot make it happen. The prodigal son relocated to a distant land to prevent any familial messaging. Indeed, the father probably did not know where his son lived. But when he allowed it by returning the father certainly spoke with his son. We are social beings and relationship is key. Familial relationships are foundational and when possible, maintaining them is paramount.

By far the most important thing to glean is to know for sure that you as well as your transgender familial member have a close, personal, intimate, and growing relationship with the Father. If either you and/or your transgender familial member have never admitted to the Lord the fact of your own personal sinfulness and asked Him to forgive you on the basis of Jesus' atoning death, please do so now. It is the greatest decision anyone will ever make. If either or both of you do have a relationship with the Father but have let it slide, you have not lost your salvation, but the joy is gone. Repent of it and return to the one who died for you. Allow Him to take control of your very being, spend time in the Word, and obey whatever He tells you. Permit God to do His transforming work in your heart and/or the heart of your transgendered loved one. See how He can mend the brokenhearted, clean the vilest sinner, forgive the most heinous sin and provide the peace that passes understanding.

GLOSSARY

M any of these definitions are tentative at best and not universally accepted. Rapid change, broad discrepancies as well as significant differences of opinion within the field of sexual non-conformity create a highly charged atmosphere that essentially precludes widely approved meanings and definitions. Nevertheless, the terms may be helpful for those unfamiliar with the transgender identity, transsexual identity, non-gender conforming, and non-binary sexual expression communities. It may also be beneficial for those unacquainted with terminology utilized in evangelical circles.

Absolute Truth: The concept that something is always trustworthy, accurate, and valid without respect to time, place, circumstance, culture, or society. It is complete, immutable, and permanent.

Ally: A person who identifies as "straight" but supports people in the LGBTQQIAAP+ community.

Agape: A Greek term translated love. It refers to the love that Christ has for humanity, *Agape* is based not on what people can do in return but upon the Father Himself. It is truly altruistic.

Asexual: An individual who is not attracted sexually to any person of either sex or gender.

Believer: An individual who accepts by faith the atoning sacrifice of the Lord Jesus as the full and complete payment for sin. A believer has an eternal relationship with the Father and holds a high view of Scripture. It is another term for saint.

Bisexual: An individual who is attracted sexually to people of two particular genders such as, but not limited to, men or women.

Christian: An individual who has made a cognitive, willful and deliberate choice to acknowledge their own personal sinfulness to God and accepted by faith Christ's atoning death on the cross as the sole sacrifice for those sins. Christian is interchanged with terms such as evangelical, believer, and saint.

Cis: An element of Latin used as a prefix to form a compound word that means on the near side of a place, object, or person. Cisalpine, cisatlantic, and ciscaucasia are three examples. In this context it is used by itself to refer to someone who is not transgender or transsexual.

Cisgender: An individual whose emotional, intellectual, social, and psychological gender is congruent with their birth sex. Sometimes these are referred to as cissexuals or simply cis.

Cisheteronormative or **cis heteronormative:** A term that means heterosexuality, predicated on the gender binary, is the norm or default sexual orientation. Non heterosexuals sometimes view this term as discriminatory.

Complementarianism: The teaching that masculinity and femininity are ordained by God. Men and women are created to complement, or complete, each other.

Cross-dresser: An individual (usually male) who wears clothing that society considers appropriate for the opposite sex. This individual is generally less likely to go public than is a transvestite.

Cultural Christians: Individuals who may call themselves Christians because they live in what they perceive to be a Christian society or culture. They may or may not belong to a church and participate in its activities but they have no personal relationship with the Father through the Son.

Cultural relativism: The concept that truth is not absolute but relative to time, place, circumstance, society, and culture in particular. What may be true in one culture at one time may not be true in the same culture at a different time or in a different culture.

Dualism: The philosophy popularized by Descartes and others that claimed humans were composed only of soul (mind, personality) and body (physical) with no eternal component. It is here contrasted with the notion of trialism which argues for the existence of body, soul, and spirit.

Evangelical: An individual who accepts several theological positions such as Conversionism, the belief that lives need to be transformed through a "born-again" experience and a lifelong process of following Jesus; Activism, the expression and demonstration of the gospel in missionary and social reform efforts; Biblicism, a high regard for and obedience to the Bible as the ultimate authority; and Crucicentrism, a stress on the sacrifice of Jesus Christ on the cross as making possible the redemption of humanity. It is used interchangeably with Christian, saint, and believer.

Father: The first person of the God Head, Trinity or Triune God.

Femmes: A term that refers to people with a destination gender that is feminine of center. It is also a French term coined in the 1950s that refers to a lesbian who uses any methods available to feminize herself and other women exclusively.

GLAAD: An acronym generally agreed to denote "Gay and (or &) Lesbian Alliance Against Defamation." Some, however, assert that the first A refers to association while the D may represent discrimination. A different take accepted by some is "Gay and Lesbian Advocates and Defenders."

Gay: A term often used in lieu of homosexual. It usually refers to males attracted sexually to other males.

Gender: The state of a person's emotional, intellectual, social, and/or psychological mindset that is male or female or any amalgamation of them in relation to the social and cultural roles considered appropriate for men or women. Essentially, it means with what sex (male, female, or some combination thereof) does an individual perceive themself?

Gender dysphoria: When an individual's emotional, intellectual, social, and psychological sexual identity differs from their birth sex. This condition was formerly known as gender identity disorder.

Gender fluidity: The ability to become knowingly and without coercion one or many of a limitless number of genders, for any length of time, at any rate of change. Gender fluidity recognizes no borders or rules of gender.

Gender non-conforming: People who do not adhere to social norms regarding dress and activities for people that are based on their biological sex and/or gender assignment. A gender non-conforming person may choose to present as neither clearly male, nor clearly female, but rather as a gender-free individual.

Holy Spirit: The third person of the God Head, Trinity or Triune God. He indwells believers from the instant of salvation until their physical demise.

Homosexual: An individual who is attracted sexually only to people of one's own sex.

Humanism: A philosophy that normally rejects supernaturalism and a spiritual component of life but stresses an individual's dignity, worth, goodness, and capacity for self-realization through reason and scientific inquiry.

Ideation: Creating and thinking about acting upon certain thoughts or ideas. Here it refers to forming the thought of suicide and perhaps a plan to carry it out as well.

Intersex: Individuals born with any of several variations in sex characteristics including chromosomes, gonads, sex hormones, or genitals that, according to the United Nations Office of the High Commissioner for Human Rights, "do not fit the typical definitions for male or female bodies." Such variations may involve genital ambiguity and combinations of chromosomal genotype and sexual phenotype other than XY-male and XX-female.

Jehovah: One of three names used for God in the Old Testament. It is based upon the Hebrew word *YHWH*, or *Yahweh*. In English translations it is normally rendered LORD.

LGBTTQQIAAP+: An ever-changing acronym for which the letters generally represent lesbian, gay, bisexual, transgender, transsexual, queer, questioning, intersex, asexual, allies, and pansexuals. The + can refer to others not yet recognized or perhaps love, acceptance, inclusion, and the embracing of all.

Lesbian: A term often used in lieu of homosexual. It normally refers to a female who is sexually attracted to other females.

Lucifer: A name for the devil or Satan. The wicked one, the liar, the father of lies, and the deceiver are a few other titles for Satan located throughout Scripture and the text.

Multidisciplinary: A term that describes the involvement of several academic disciplines or professional specializations in discussing a topic.

Non-binary sexual expression: One term used to describe individuals who may experience or exhibit a gender or sexual identity that is neither exclusively male nor female, but is between or transcends genders or sexes. People may identify as gender fluid, agender (without gender), third gender, or something else entirely.

Pansexual: An individual whose sexual attraction is not based on gender and may themselves be fluid when it comes to gender or sexual identity.

Pluralism: A philosophy that argues for diversity among belief systems, worldviews, mindsets, and perspectives. It states that the various components strengthen a culture or society.

Queer: An umbrella term used by the LGBT+ or LGBTTQQIAAP+ community that denotes or relates to a sexual or gender identity that does not correspond to established ideas of sexuality and gender.

Questioning: Used to refer to someone who is still unsure or are still exploring his/her/their gender and/or sexual identity.

Quiltbag: An acronym that generally refers to: QUeer, QUestioning, Intersex, Lesbian, Transgender, Bisexual, Asexual, Agender, Gay, Gender queer. Its chief purpose is to replace the constantly revising letters **LGBTTQQIAAP+.** Some, however, want to add the term "folks" to make it sound more inclusive while others view it as derogatory.

Saint: Any person who has chosen to place his or her trust for eternal salvation solely in the atoning death, burial, and resurrection of the Lord Jesus. A saint is from the time of salvation, indwelt by the Holy Spirit. It is another term for believer, evangelical, or Christian.

Scripture: The sacred writings of the Old and New Testaments. It is also referred to as the Bible as well as Holy Writ. It is the foundation of Christianity.

Sex: An individual's chromosomal makeup that determines their biological means of reproduction. Whether one is organically male or female is determined at conception.

Son: The second person of the God Head, Trinity, or Triune God. He is also known as Jesus or the Christ.

Transgender: An individual whose sexual identity does not conform unambiguously to conventional or biological ideas of male or female.

They have a gender identity or gender expression that differs from their birth sex.

Transgender Identity: A state or condition in which a person's uniqueness does not conform unambiguously to conventional or biological ideas of male or female. They express themselves on a gender continuum that differs from their birth six.

Transsexual: An individual who senses intellectually, emotionally, socially, and/or psychologically that they are truly the opposite of their biological sex.

Transsexual Identity: A state or condition in which a person has a prolonged, persistent desire to relinquish their primary and secondary sex characteristics and acquire those of the opposite sex. It particularly describes persons who go so far as to live as members of the other sex through dress, hormonal treatments, or surgical reassignment.

Transvestite: An individual who wears clothing along with accessories and often adopts mannerisms society considers appropriate for the opposite sex. This person is more likely to go public than is a cross-dresser.

Trialism: The philosophy that claims humans are comprised of body, soul, and spirit. It is here contrasted with the notion of dualism which includes only body and soul but denies the existence of an eternal component.

ANNOTATED BIBLIOGRAPHY

SCRIPTURE

Ryrie, Charles Caldwell. *The Ryrie Study Bible New American Standard Version*. Chicago: Moody Press, 1995. All Scripture passages in this book are quoted from the New American Standard Bible, 1995 revision. There are many fine translations available such as, but not limited to, *Holman Christian Standard*, *King James*, *New King James*, *Amplified Bible* and the *English Standard Version*. Nevertheless, the *New American Standard* is considered by many to be the most literal of modern translations. First released in full in 1971, the text was revised in 1995 and a new one is scheduled for 2020.

Stanley, Charles F. ed. *Life Principles Bible New American Standard Version*. Nashville: Thomas Nelson, 2005. This study Bible focuses readers on 30 essential principles found in Scripture. It incorporates numerous verses along with voluminous insights to illustrate those concepts and how effectively to apply them to one's daily life and walk with the Lord.

MONOGRAPHS

Cairns, Earle E. *Christianity Through the Centuries: A History of the Christian Church.* Zondervan Publishing House: Grand Rapids, 1981. Although seriously dated the late Cairns' work is highly regarded by many historians. A long time professor at Wheaton College his work might be considered by some to be right of center.

Carson, D. A. *The Gagging of God: Christianity Confronts Pluralism.* Zondervan: Grand Rapids, 1996. ePub ed. 2009. D. A. (Donald Arthur) Carson's monograph is essential reading for anyone interested in examining Western philosophical developments of the previous two centuries. He incorporates an impeccable biblical understanding along with the growing popularity of secularism with its specious foundation of pragmatism, cultural relativism, and pluralism.

Crabb, Larry. *Fully Alive: A Biblical Vision of Gender that Frees Men and Women to Live Beyond Stereotypes.* Grand Rapids: Baker Books, 2013. Crabb is a noted psychologist, author, as well as founder and executive administrator of New Way Ministries. The Spiritual Director for the American Association of Christian Counselors, Crabb has, since 1996, been the distinguished scholar in residence of Colorado Christian University.

Erickson, Millard J. *Christian Theology.* Grand Rapids: Baker Books, 1993. This classic systematic text is used widely in evangelical colleges and seminaries. Erickson, an ordained Baptist minister, is a fairly conservative evangelical and only moderately Calvinistic. He is accommodating of alternate views on a number of issues, but remains one of the more vocal opponents of the most liberal side of evangelicalism, open theism and postmodernism.

Foner, Eric. *Give Me Liberty: An American History, 4th Brief Ed.* New York: W. W. Norton, 2014. This classic American history text by the highly acclaimed Eric Foner, DeWitt Clinton professor of history at Columbia University, provides helpful background material regarding American historical and religious context. He writes extensively on American political history as well as the history of freedom, among other topics. Foner's work has a definite leftist slant, perhaps due in part to the fact that his father and paternal uncles were active in the labor union movements either as participants or as historians.

Gaustad, Edwin Scott. *A Religious History of America, rev. ed.* San Francisco: Harper Collins, 1990. Although dated, Gaustad's monograph is a highly acclaimed publication that accomplishes its purpose "to portray the role of religion in all stages of this country's development—from the moment that America was only a gleam in the eye of an Italian sailor to the full-blown and often bewildering present."

Hofstadter, Richard. *Social Darwinism in American Thought.* Boston: Beacon Press, 1992. Hofstadter masterfully portrays the extensive influence of Darwinism on American social theory. Furthermore, he explores the conflict between thinkers regarding the implications of evolutionary theory for social thought and political action. Much like his contemporary Edmund Morgan, Hofstadter's work reflected a conservative mindset.

Kelly, Gary. *Sexuality Today, 10th ed.* New York: McGraw-Hill, 2009. According to his website, Gary Kelly's sexuality education work with students received national recognition with his election to the board of directors of the Sexuality Information and Education Council of the United States (SIECUS). Kelly served for eight years as editor of the Journal of Sex Education and Therapy and was one of the charter editorial board members of the American Journal of Sexuality Education. He is a member of the American Association of Sexuality Educators, Counselors, and Therapists and of the Society for the Scientific Study of Human Sexuality. He has written several books, including this college text. It maintains a decidedly secular position clearly to the sociocultural left.

Lloyd-Jones, D. Martyn *The Christian Soldier: An Exposition of Ephesians 6:10-13* 3rd printing. Grand Rapids: Baker Books, 2003.

_____. *The Christian Soldier: An Exposition of Ephesians 6:10-20* Grand Rapids: Baker Books, 1983. David Martyn Lloyd-Jones was a Welsh medical doctor turned pastor. He preached 30 years at the London Westminster Chapel, an Independent Evangelical Church. His books are essentially expository sermons, many were published posthumously. He held a high view of Scripture

Livesay, Harold. *Andrew Carnegie and the Rise of Big Business, 3rd ed.* Mark C. Carnes, ed. Hoboken: Pearson, 2007. A specialist in American business history, Harold Livesay was professor of history at Texas A&M University. His book explores the life and legacy of Andrew Carnegie, one of the greatest captains of industry and philanthropists in the history of the United States. As a man who spent his early career in various business enterprises, his work reflects a relatively pro-business and conservative perspective.

Morgan, Edmund S. *The Puritan Dilemma, The Story of John Winthrop, 3rd ed.* Mark C. Carnes, ed. Hoboken: Pearson, 2006. Morgan, an American historian and an eminent authority on early American history, was the Sterling Emeritus Professor of History at Yale University, where he taught from 1955 to 1986. He specialized in American colonial history, including Puritanism and its role in American religious and philosophical thought. Morgan's research and writing reveal that he was a product of his generation when historians reflected a conservative persuasion.

Pepper, Rachel ed. *Transitions of the Heart*. Berkeley: Cleis Press, 2012. This book of vignettes appears innocuous as it contains various stories of parents (usually mothers) with their transgender children and how the family dealt with the situation. Nevertheless, Cleis Press is an independent publisher of materials regarding erotica, gay and lesbian studies, feminism, gender studies, among other related subjects. It reflects a leftist perspective.

Reece, Barry L. and Monique E. Reece. *Effective Human Relations: Interpersonal and Organizational Applications 13th ed*. Boston: Cengage Learning, 2017. This textbook provides, among other things, suggestions to improve relationships. The book claims that the most important is the relationship with oneself. Mastering intrapersonal and interpersonal interaction, connection, and communication skills facilitates one's self-confidence, self-efficacy, and self-esteem. Barry L. Reece is professor emeritus at Virginia Polytechnic Institute and State University. Prior to joining the faculty at Virginia Tech, he held positions at Ellsworth Community College and the University of Northern Iowa. He is the author or coauthor of several college textbooks. Monique E. Reece is an author, teacher, and consultant. She was an affiliated executive faculty at the Institute for Leadership and Organizational Performance at the University of Denver, teaching in both the executive MB and professional MBA programs. Its position is relatively centrist.

Salazar, Lisa. *Transparently: Behind the Scenes of a Good Life*. Self-published, 2011. This fast-reading memoir details much of the emotional rollercoaster that Santiago – Jim – Lisa Salazar experienced from the early years in Colombia to the teen years in California and later as an adult in British Columbia. Although peppered with religious terminology, Salazar never refers to a personal, growing, intimate relationship with the Father. Nor is there any mention of trusting Christ as personal Savior. It provides a picture of an individual who lived as a heterosexual man, married, and sired three boys. Later he transitioned into a woman, first with hormones followed by gender reassignment surgery. It does provide an insightful picture into someone who dealt with gender dysphoria in perhaps the most extreme way. It is left of center, particularly in its religious perspective.

Singer, C. Gregg. *A Theological Interpretation of American History*, *rev. ed*. Vestavia, AL: Solid Ground Christian Books, 2009. Although dated, the monograph provides a thorough description and analysis of major theological movements that held sway from Colonial America through World War II. He clearly delineates the close ties between theology, philosophy, history, and political developments. Indeed, he claimed that only "in the light of the Christian revelation can American history be brought into proper perspective. Clearly, it is required reading for any serious analysis of American history, philosophy, religion, or politics. It holds to a right of center persuasion.

Stanley, Charles. *The Blessings of Brokenness: Why God Allows Us to Go Through Hard Times*. Grand Rapids: Zondervan, 1997. Based in part upon personal experiences, Stanley explains why God permits believers to experience pain and suffering. Furthermore he describes how the Lord uses those difficulties to mold saints into the image of the Lord Jesus.

Veith, Gene Edward, Jr., *Postmodern Times: A Christian Guide to*

Contemporary Thought and Culture. Wheaton: Crossway Books, 1994. Veith, a scholar, author, and professor of literature emeritus, was also dean of Academic Affairs and Provost at Patrick Henry College. Formerly the culture editor of *World* magazine, an evangelical Christian biweekly publication, Veith remains director of the Cranach Institute, a research and educational arm of Concordia Theological Seminary. Its analysis is right of center.

Walker, Williston, Richard A. Norris, David W. Lotz, and Robert T. Handy. *A History of the Christian Church,* 4th *ed.* New York: MacMillan Publishing Company, 1985. This book, although dated, is highly regarded by many. Its authors are widely published with impeccable educational and professorial accolades. The book is written from a left of center perspective.

Zinn, Howard. *A People's History of the United States.* New York: Harper Perennial Modern Classics, 2003. An avowed socialist, the late Howard Zinn was clearly left wing in his historical perspective. He took an unsympathetic view toward evangelicalism. In his review, Eric Foner noted that Zinn's book was the only volume to tell America's story from the point of view of—and in the words of—America's women factory workers, African Americans, Native Americans, working poor, and immigrant laborers.

REFERENCE WORKS

Green, Jay P., ed. *The Interlinear Hebrew-Greek-English Bible*, 2nd ed. Peabody: Hendrickson Publishers, 1985 reprint 2007. Green was originally a typewriter salesman for Remington, and as a young adult accepted Christ as his Savior. Most of the rest of his life was dedicated to Bible translating and publishing. Perhaps the most important driving force in his translating work came from his daughter who asked him to make a Bible easier to understand than the King James Version. He held a high view of Scripture and this work includes a literal translation from the Aramaic, Hebrew, and Greek. Its second edition includes the Strong's numbering system.

Strong, James. *Strong's Exhaustive Concordance* Nashville: Abingdon Press, 1974, 32nd printing. Strong was a nineteenth century biblical scholar whose most notable accomplishment was his concordance issued in 1890, three years before his death. In this work every Hebrew and Greek word in Scripture was numbered, parsed, and defined. Each was then cross referenced with the English word in the King James Version. It remains an invaluable tool for a biblical scholar who takes a high view of Scripture.

Vine, W. E., Merrill F. Unger, and William White, Jr. eds. *Vines Expository Dictionary of Biblical Words rev. ed.* Vine produced his original work in 1940 to assist pastors and scholars in their study of biblical languages. He held a high view of Scripture. Unger, a Baptist pastor and biblical scholar held a high view of Scripture and assisted Vine in the original work. White, also one with a high view of Scripture edited the newer edition to incorporate recent archeological discoveries such as Ebla along with modern scholarship in ancient languages.

BLOGS

https://transblog.grieve-smith.com/2016/08/23/my-catalog-of-woes – Angus/Andrea Grieve Smith is a non-transitioning transgender. This blog contains some exceptionally helpful perceptions regarding differences within the transgender community.

https://www.transgendermap.com is associated with Andrea James and describes itself as a "free website [that] shows how to make a gender transition." Furthermore, "it tells about gender identity and gender expression, as well as the social, legal, and medical ways to make a transgender transition."

https://zagria.blogspot.com describes itself as "A Gender Variance Who's Who." It includes essays on trans, intersex, cis, and other persons and topics from a trans perspective.... All human life is here. This site is the most comprehensive on the web devoted to trans history and biography. Well over 1,400 persons worthy of note, both famous and obscure, are discussed in detail, and many more are mentioned in passing.

WEBSITES

https://4thwavenow.com/ 4thWaveNow was started by the mother of a teenage girl who suddenly announced she was a "trans man" after a few weeks of total immersion in YouTube transition vlogs and other trans-oriented social media. (The daughter has since desisted from identifying as transgender.) After much research and fruitless searching for an alternative online viewpoint, this mom began writing about her deepening skepticism of the ever-accelerating medical and media fascination with the phenomenon of "transgender children." 4thWaveNow has expanded to feature not only the writing of the website's founder, but also that of other parents, formerly trans-identified people, and people with professional expertise and experience with young people questioning their gender identity. It appears right of center philosophically.

https://liveabout.com is a website that claims to "take great pride in the quality of our content. We produce fact-based, unbiased, well-researched articles that acknowledge the validity of all viewpoints." Nevertheless, it is highly sympathetic with sexual non-conformity.

http://www.religioustolerance.org/ is the website of the Ontario Consultants on Religious Tolerance. According to its website, "everyone is very welcome here…whether you describe yourself as an agnostic, animist, atheist, bitheist, deist, duotheist, evangelical, fundamentalist, neo-pagan, a NOTA (i.e., NOT Affiliated or NONE), pagan, polytheist, progressive, religious conservative, religious liberal, secular humanist, secularist, spiritual but not religious, theist, unitarian, wiccan, Zoroastrian, etc., or some combination of the above." Furthermore, their "main goal is to discuss the beliefs and practices of all of these groups—and others—fairly and accurately, and to promote religious tolerance, acceptance, knowledge, cooperation, understanding, and coexistence." Its position is left of center.

https://reset.me provides journalism on natural therapies and medicines to enhance the mind, body, and spirit. Reset strives to help expand consciousness and spread more love around the world. The team behind Reset.me endeavors to build a community that connects like-minded individuals worldwide to promote the sharing of knowledge and experiences. Reset your mind. Reset your life.

http://sciencedaily.com is an American website launched in 1995. It publishes edited press releases but apparently has at best a minimal research staff.

https://thebestbrainpossible.com is a website hosted by Debbie Hampton. She writes that following "decades of depression, a serious suicide attempt and resulting brain injury, I not only survived, but went on to thrive by discovering the super power we all have to build a better brain and joyful life. If I can do it, you can too. Let me inspire and inform you to do the same. No brain injury required."

https://transequality.org is the website for The National Center for Transgender Equality. According to its mission statement, the organization promotes "change in policy and society to increase understanding and acceptance of transgender people. In the nation's capital and throughout the country, NCTE works to replace disrespect, discrimination, and violence with empathy, opportunity, and justice." Its sociopolitical sympathies are leftist.

PEER-REVIEWED JOURNALS

BioMed Research International is a peer-reviewed open-access scientific journal covering all aspects of biomedical sciences. It was established in 2001 as the *Journal of Biomedicine and Biotechnology* with Abdelali Haoudi as first editor in chief. The journal obtained its current title in 2013 and is published by Hindawi Publishing Corporation.

Foh, Susan T. "What is the Woman's Desire?" *The Westminster Theological Journal.* Volume 37 (1974/75). According to its inaugural publication, the journal was "founded upon the conviction that the Holy Scriptures are the word of God and the only infallible rule of faith and practice, and that the system of belief commonly designated the Reformed Faith is the purest and most consistent formulation and expression of the system of truth set forth in the Holy Scriptures." The journal exists to further Reformed theological scholarship and through it to serve the ministers and members of Presbyterian and Reformed churches. Susan T. Foh is an American biblical scholar with degrees from Wellesley College and Westminster Theological Seminary. She is the author of *Women and the Word of God: A Response to Biblical Feminism*. In it she argues that the "desire" mentioned in Genesis 3:16 is actually a desire to dominate.

Hess, J., R. Rossi Neto, L. Panic, H. Rubben, and W. Senf. "Satisfaction with Male-to-Female Gender Reassignment Surgery: Results of a Retrospective Analysis." *Dtsch Arztebl Int*. 2014; 111(0047):795–801. *Deutsches* Ärzteblatt *International* is a bilingual weekly online journal of clinical medicine and public health. Its self-description reads "As the official journal of the German Medical Association and the National Association of Statutory Health Insurance Physicians, we publish independent, peer-reviewed articles from all branches of clinical medicine. In addition, you will find editorials and a section devoted to scientific discussion (correspondence). We hope that for our international readership our journal will be both an important source of medical information and a window to the German medical scene." Hess is a scientist with a research interest in the quality of life enjoyed by those who have had sex reassignment surgery. He tends to focus on the notion that gender confirmation surgery provides relief for transgenders.

Kawa, Shadia and James Giordano. "A Brief Historicity of the Diagnostic and Statistical Manual of Mental Disorders: Issues and Implications for the Future of Psychiatric Canon and Practice." *Philosophy, Ethics, and Humanities in Medicine* January 13, 2012. doi:10.1186/1747-5341-7-2. *Philosophy, Ethics, and Humanities in Medicine* considers articles on the philosophy of medicine and biology, and on ethical aspects of clinical practice and research. *Philosophy, Ethics, and Humanities in Medicine* is an open-access, peer-reviewed online journal that encompasses all aspects of the philosophy of medicine and biology, and the ethical aspects of clinical practice and research. It also considers papers at the intersection of medicine and humanities, including the history of medicine, that are relevant to contemporary philosophy of medicine and bioethics.

Melloni, Carlo. "Management of Gender Dysphoria and Creation of a Gender Team." *Journal of Reconstructive Surgery and Anaplastology* Vol. 5, Issue 2, 2016 5:117. The *Journal of Anaplastology and Reconstructive Surgery* is an open-access, interdisciplinary journal covering all the reconstructive and aesthetic aspects within the field. According to the website, the "journal aims to bring up-to-the-minute reports on the latest techniques and follow-up for all areas of reconstructive surgery and anaplastology." It "provides a forum to exchange ideas between surgical procedures with audit and outcome studies of new and established techniques in the field including: cleft lip and palate and other heads and neck surgery, hand surgery, lower limb trauma, burns, skin cancer, breast surgery and aesthetic surgery." Editor Carlo Melloni's research interests are in aesthetic surgery (especially rhinoplasty), reconstructive surgery, genital and perineal surgery and gender reassignment surgery (MTF and FTM).

Meybodi Mazaheri A, A. Hajebi, A. Ghanbari Jolfaei. "The Frequency of Personality Disorders in Patients with Gender Identity Disorder." *Medical Journal of the Islamic Republic of Iran*, September 10, 2014 Vol. 28:90. The *Medical Journal of the Islamic Republic of Iran (MJIRI)* is an editorially independent, peer-reviewed online open-access journal owned and published by Iran University of Medical Sciences and aims to be a publication of international repute for reporting current regional and international adventures in all aspects of the medicine. Azadeh Mazaheri Meybodi is an assistant professor of psychiatry at the Minimally Invasive

Surgery Research Center, Iran University of Medical Sciences, Tehran, Iran. Her interests include personality disorder and gender identity disorder or gender dysphoria. Ahmed Hajebi, a prolific scholar, is professor of psychiatry in the Department of Psychiatry and Psychology Research Center at the University of Tehran, Tehran, Iran. An accomplished academician and practitioner, Atefeh Ghanbari Jolfaei is head of the psychiatric ward and director of transcranial magnetic stimulation program at Rasoul Akram hospital in Tehran, Iran.

Mohammadi, Mohammad-Reza, Ali Khalegi. "Transsexualism: A Different Viewpoint to Brain Changes," *Clinical Psychopharmacology and Neuroscience* 2018, 16(2): 136–143. *Clinical Psychopharmacology and Neuroscience*, launched in 2003, is the official journal of The Korean College of Neuropsychopharmacology (KCNP), and the associate journal for Asian College of Neuropsychopharmacology (AsCNP). According to its website, the journal "aims to publish evidence-based, scientifically written articles related to clinical and preclinical studies in the field of psychopharmacology and neuroscience." Furthermore, it aspires to "foster and encourage communications between psychiatrist, neuroscientist, and all related experts in Asia as well as worldwide." Mohammad-Reza Mohammadi is a professor and researcher of psychiatry at the Roozbeh hospital at the Tehran University of Medical Sciences. Ali Khalegi is a researcher in the Department of Psychiatry and Psychology Research Center at the University of Tehran, Tehran, Iran.

Philosophy, Ethics, and Humanities in Medicine is the official publication of the Pellegrino Center for Clinical Bioethics at Georgetown University Medical Center. Shadia Kawa is closely associated with the Division of Cancer Control and Population Sciences, Basic Biobehavioral and Psychological Sciences Branch, Behavioral Research Program, National Cancer Institute. James Giordano, PhD, MPhil, is professor in the Departments of Neurology and Biochemistry, chief of the Neuroethics Studies Program of the Pellegrino Center for Clinical Bioethics, and co-director of the O'Neill-Pellegrino Program in Brain Science and Global Health Law and Policy at Georgetown University Medical Center, Washington, D.C., USA. He is also a distinguished visiting professor of brain science, health promotions and ethics at the Coburg University of Applied Sciences, Coburg, Germany, and was formerly 2011–2012 JW Fulbright Foundation visiting professor of neurosciences and neuroethics at the Ludwig-Maximilians University, Munich, Germany.

Saraswat, Aruna, Jamie Weinand, and Joshua Safer. "Evidence Supporting the Biologic Nature of Gender Identity." *Endocrine Practice* February, 2015. DOI: 10.4158/EP14351.RA. *Endocrine Practice* – The Journal for Clinical Endocrinologists, the American Association of Clinical Endocrinologist's (AACE) official journal, is peer-reviewed, published twelve times a year, and contains original articles, review articles, commentaries, editorials, and visual vignettes. Clinical endo-crinologists worldwide rely on *Endocrine Practice* to stay on the leading edge of treatment of patients with endocrine diseases. Aruna A Saraswat, MD, has practiced medicine for eleven years primarily in Boston, MA. Her specialties include internal medicine and endocrinology, diabetes and metabolism. She is also an assistant professor at Tufts University School of Medicine Department. Joshua Safer is executive director of the Mount Sinai Center for Transgender Medicine and Surgery in New York. Previously, he was the inaugural medical director of the Center for Transgender Medicine and Surgery at Boston Medical Center. He is also senior faculty at the Icahn School of Medicine at Mount Sinai. Dr. Safer received his medical degree from the University of Wisconsin. He completed his internal medicine residency at Mount Sinai Beth Israel Medical Center in New York City and his endocrinology fellowship at Beth Israel Deaconess Medical Center in Boston. Dr. Safer is the president of the United States Professional Association for Transgender Health (USPATH) and steering committee co-chair of the international transgender research consortium, TransNet, which seeks to develop national research strategy in transgender medicine. In addition, he is a past president of the Association of Specialty Professors, the umbrella organization for leaders in internal medicine subspecialty education, and a past secretary-treasurer of the Association of Program Directors in Endocrinology and Metabolism (APDEM). Dr. Safer is a co-author of the 2017 Endocrine Society guidelines for the medical care of transgender patients. He also serves on the Global Education Initiative committee for the World Professional Association for Transgender Health (WPATH), on the Standards of Care revision committee for WPATH, and as a scientific co-chair for WPATH's international meeting. Dr. Safer's research focus has been to demonstrate health and quality of life benefits accruing from increased access to care for transgender patients. His current and past sources of funding support include the NIH and a number of private foundations. Thus, one can easily determine Safer's bias toward the acceptance of a biological etiology of transgender identity.

Servick, Kelly. "Study of Gay Brothers may confirm X chromosome link to homosexuality." *Science*, November 17, 2014. *Science* magazine is a peer-reviewed academic journal of the American Association for the Advancement of Science. Based in Washington, D.C., it was established in 1880 and publishes science-related news and opinions on science policy. Kelly Servick is a staff writer at *Science*. She focuses on stories about biomedical research and policy. Her work has appeared on KUSP radio, Wired.com, *Scientific American*, and other outlets.

Spack, Norman P. and Stephanie A Roberts. "Caring for Transgender Youth." *Journal of Yoga and Physical Therapy* Vol. 5 Issue 4 January 2015 doi:10.4172/2157-7595.1000213. The *Journal of Yoga and Physical Therapy* is an open-access, peer-reviewed medical journal that aims to publish the most complete and reliable source of information on the discoveries and current developments in the mode of original articles, review articles, case reports, short communications, etc. in all areas of the yoga and physical therapy-like types of yoga, physiotherapy, sports science, exercise science, rehabilitation, meditation, and related subjects like physical medicine, sports medicine, fitness and aerobics, and making them freely available worldwide through scholarly publishing. Norman Spack is an American pediatric endocrinologist at Boston Children's Hospital, where he co-founded the hospital's Gender Management Service clinic in February 2007. It is America's first clinic to treat transgender children. He is an internationally known specialist in treatment for intersexed and transgender youth, and is one of the first doctors in the United States who advocates prescribing hormone replacement therapy to minors. Stephanie Roberts is a pediatric endocrinologist at Boston Children's Hospital.

PERIODICALS

The Atlantic is an American magazine founded in 1857 by such notables as Ralph Waldo Emerson, Harriet Beecher Stowe, and Henry

Wadsworth Longfellow, among several others. It covers politics, health, culture, science, technology, news, and various other topics. Its political bias is clearly to the left. Ed Yong is a science journalist based in Washington, D.C., who reports for *The Atlantic*.

Boston University Medical Center, "Transgender: Evidence on the biological nature of gender identity," *Science Daily*, February 13, 2015. Sciencedaily.com is an American website launched in 1995. It publishes edited press releases but apparently has at best a minimal research staff.

Duke, Selwyn. "The Transgender Con? Many 'Transgender People Regret Switch,'" *The New American*, November 11, 2014, republished 2017. *The New American,* founded in 1985, publishes well-researched articles on political, social, and cultural topics. Its editorial stance leans to the right. Selwyn Duke is a traditionalist media personality whose work has been published widely online and in print, appearing at outlets such as *The Hill*, *The American Conservative*, *WorldNetDaily* and *American Thinker*.

Hamzelou, Jessica. "Gay or straight? Saliva test can predict male sexual orientation." *New Scientist*, October 8, 2015. *New Scientist*, founded in 1956, claims to be the world's most popular weekly science and technology magazine. It focuses primarily on issues especially relevant to the United Kingdom, the United States, and Australia. Jessica Hamzelou is a biomed and health reporter at *New Scientist*.

Lewis, Ricki. "Here's what we really know about transgender genetics—so far." Genetic Literacy Project, March 29, 2018 (accessed July 17, 2019). Ricki Lewis is a science writer with a PhD in genetics. She has written life science college textbooks for many years and countless articles.

See more on the Genetic Literacy Project under Scholarly Studies in the annotated bibliography.

Mills, Melinda. "Perspective Genomics: How do genes affect same-sex behavior?" *Science.* August 30, 2019, Vol. 365, Issue 6456, pp. 869–870. Mills, a Canadian and Dutch demographer and sociologist, is the Nuffield professor and director of the Leverhulme Centre for Demographic Science at Nuffield College and the University of Oxford. Her research spans a range of interdisciplinary topics at the intersection of demography, sociology, molecular genetics, and statistics. Her substantive research specializes in fertility and human reproductive behavior, assortative mating, chronotypes, labor market, life course, and inequality. She does contend for a genetic causation for homosexuality.

Morabito, Stella. "Trouble in Transtopia: Murmurs of Sex Change Regret." *The Federalist.* November 11, 2014. *The Federalist* is a web magazine that focuses on American culture, politics, government policy, and religion. It has a conservative or perhaps even libertarian bent, encouraging a traditional worldview. Stella Morabito is a senior contributor at *The Federalist.* Her essays have also appeared in the *Washington Examiner, American Thinker, Public Discourse, Human Life Review* as well as *The New Oxford Review.*

Reed, Anne. "From transgendered to transformed." *American Family Association Journal.* December 2018. The *American Family Association Journal* is the official publication of the American Family Association. The organization's mission is to inform, equip, and activate individuals to strengthen the moral foundations of American culture, and give aid to the church here and abroad in its task of fulfilling the Great Commission. Anne Reed is an award-winning writer for the American

Family Association's print magazine and blog. Her writing is founded on Scripture and often warns believers of deception making its way into the church.

Trotter, Daniel. "Born this way? Researchers explore the science of gender identity." *Science News* August 3, 2017. For almost a century, *Science News* journalists have covered advances in science, medicine, and technology for the general public, including the 1925 Scopes "monkey" trial, the advent of the atomic age in 1945, the space race, and the revolution of genetic engineering from the discovery of DNA to today's gene-editing technology. It was founded as an independent non-profit in 1921 by newspaper magnate E.W. Scripps and zoologist W.E. Ritter, who wanted to improve the quality and accuracy of science journalism. Daniel Trotter was a reporter for *Science News*.

Williams, Shawna. "Are the Brains of Transgender People Different from Those of Cisgender People?" *The Scientist*, March 12, 2018. Shawna Williams is a freelance writer based in Baltimore, Maryland. *The Scientist* is the magazine for life science professionals—a publication dedicated to covering a wide range of topics central to the study of cell and molecular biology, genetics, and other life science fields.

SCHOLARLY PRESENTATIONS, ADDRESSES

Green, Richard. "Is Being Transgender Genetically Determined at Conception?" Address delivered to the Ontario Consultants on Religious Tolerance. December 18, 2017. Richard Green was an American-British sexologist, psychiatrist, lawyer, and author specializing in homosexuality and transsexualism, specifically gender identity disorder (gender dysphoria) in children. See more on the Ontario Consultants on Religious Tolerance under websites in the annotated bibliography.

Toufighi, Hamidreza. "A Review of Gender Dysphoria." Presentation given at the Tehran University of Medical Sciences. December, 2017. Hamidreza Toufighi is a psychiatrist, graduated and board certified from the Roozbeh hospital, Tehran University of Medical Sciences. Hamidreza is interested in research in neuro-psychoanalysis and community mental health. He is a psychiatry resident in the Psychiatry and Psychology Research Center of the Tehran University of Medical Sciences in Tehran, Iran. Gender dysphoria and its causes are among his research interests.

NOTED SCIENTISTS, PROJECTS, AND SCHOLARLY STUDIES

The National Transgender Discrimination Survey

Haas, Ann, Philip L. Rodgers and Jody Herman. "Suicide Attempts Among Transgender and Gender Non-conforming Adults Findings of the National Transgender Discrimination Survey." American Foundation for Suicide Prevention/The Williams Institute UCLA College of Law, January 2014. This misleading study attributes excessively high suicide rates of transgenders chiefly upon the discrimination they experience. However, their interpretations are highly flawed. Ann P. Haas, PhD, is the senior director of education and prevention at the American Foundation for Suicide Prevention (AFSP). Her work has focused in particular on suicide and suicide risk among teens and college students, LGBT populations, and veterans. In 2005, she co-authored the chapter on youth suicide in a volume produced by the Annenberg Foundation's Adolescent Mental Health Initiative, and was the lead author of a 2011 consensus report titled "Suicide and Suicide Risk in Lesbian, Gay, Bisexual and Transgender Populations:

Review and Recommendations," which appeared in the January 2011 edition of the *Journal of Homosexuality*. She is also on the Task Force on LGBT Populations of the National Action Alliance for Suicide Prevention. Jody L. Herman is a Williams Institute Scholar of Public Policy at UCLA School of Law. Her research has included studies of the fiscal impacts of discrimination against transgender people; employer-provided health benefits coverage for gender transition; the development of questions to identify gender minorities on population-based surveys; and minority stress, health, and suicidal ideation among transgender people. Her research focuses on measurement of gender identity in survey research and the prevalence and impact of discrimination based on gender identity or expression, including issues related to gender regulation in public space and the built environment. Herman was previously a research consultant on issues of voting rights in low-income minority communities and gender identity discrimination. Dr. Philip L. Rodgers is an evaluation scientist with the American Foundation for Suicide Prevention and manages the Best Practices Registry for Suicide Prevention in collaboration with the Suicide Prevention Resource Center. He holds a PhD in research and evaluation methodology from Utah State University.

GENETIC LITERACY PROJECT

The Genetic Literacy Project was founded in Cincinnati, OH, in 2012 by Jon Entine to promote public awareness and discussion of genetics, biotechnology, evolution, and science literacy. Its articles focus on human genetics, genetic engineering, the use and impact of crop protection chemicals and pollinator health. Jon Entine is an American science writer and consultant. He is a senior fellow at the Institute for Food and

Agricultural Literacy at the University of California, Davis, the founder and executive director of the Genetic Literacy Project, and a scholar at the American Enterprise Institute. He also provides private consulting services through ESG Mediametrics, a company he founded. After working as a network news writer and producer for NBC News and ABC News, Entine moved into scholarly research and print journalism. However, he does have critics who contend that Jon Entine is a corporate propagandist and pseudo-journalist who utilizes his media savvy to promote the opinions and positions of chemical corporations, by posing as an independent journalist. Entine has multiple documented ties to biotech companies Monsanto and Syngenta, and plays a key marketing role via another industry front group known as the American Council on Science and Health.

THE WHAT WE KNOW PROJECT

https://whatweknow.inequality.cornell.edu/about/ – The What We Know Project is an online research portal based at the Center for the Study of Inequality at Cornell University that marks a path-breaking convergence of scholarship, public policy, and new media technology. Focusing on several pressing public policy debates, What We Know brings together in one place the preponderance of scholarly evidence that informs these debates so that policymakers, journalists, researchers, and the public can make truly informed decisions about what policies and positions best serve the public interest. It is clearly biased toward the left.

SWAAB, DICK FERDINAND, MD

Swaab, Dick Ferdinand (D. F.). A Dutch physician and neurobiologist (brain researcher), Swaab is a professor of neurobiology at the University of Amsterdam and until 2005 director of the Netherlands Institute for Brain Research (Nederlands Instituut voor Hersenonderzoek) of the Royal Netherlands Academy of Arts and Sciences (Koninklijke Nederlandse Akademie van Wetenschappen). He is best known for his research and discoveries in the field of brain anatomy and physiology, in particular the impact that various hormonal and biochemical factors in the womb have on brain development. Another area of his work, which has drawn much attention, is his research on how sexual dimorphism relates to brain anatomy, as well as research relating to sexual orientation and transsexuality. Through his years of research, Swaab, according to his own words, came to the deterministic and materialistic conclusion that brains are not things we have, but rather brains are what we are: the physical and chemical processes in our brains determine how we react and who we are. Currently, he is most active in the field of depression and Alzheimer's research. His work has on several occasions produced controversy. After conducting research suggesting links between brain anatomy and sexual orientation, he reports receiving death threats from individuals believing this work was attempting to "pathologize" homosexuality and treat it as a biological abnormality or disorder. His view that neither free will nor metaphysical entities such as souls or spirits exist has also prompted negative reactions among various religious groups. He consistently defends his studies in the face of such criticism.

POSITION STATEMENT

Cretella, Michelle A. "Gender Identity Harms Children." The American College of Pediatricians position statement. The American College of Pediatricians is a socially conservative national organization of pediatricians and other healthcare professionals dedicated to the health and well-being of children. The college produces sound policy, based upon the best available research, to assist parents and to influence society in the endeavor of childrearing. Dr. Michelle A. Cretella, MD, FCP, is the president of the American College of Pediatricians. She is a board certified general pediatrician with a special interest in adolescent mental and sexual health.

SERMONS

Charles Stanley has several helpful books and sermons on various topics. For example, "Taking Control of Your Thoughts" describes how one may establish and maintain control of one's mind. Another, "Dressed for the Battle," that aired on In Touch Friday, August 2, 2019 and August 5, 2019, provides keen insight on preparing oneself for the warfare that Christians face each day.

NEWSPAPERS

Batty, David. "Mistaken Identity." *The Guardian*. July 30, 2004. Headquartered in London, *The Guardian* is a nearly 200-year-old newspaper with an American and other non-British editions. The third largest newspaper in Britain, it is clearly biased toward the left as the self-proclaimed world's leading liberal voice. David Batty is a news editor and writer. His specialist areas are the super-rich, cultural politics, visual art, higher education, and social affairs. He has written for *The Guardian* since 2001 and also lectures in journalism.

Friess, Steve. "Mike Penner, Christian Daniels: A Tragic Love Story." *Los Angeles Weekly*, August 19, 2010. According to its website, *L.A. Weekly* and laweekly.com have grown into editorial powerhouses in the dynamic

#2 market in the country. *L.A. Weekly* found success by attracting a specific desirable L.A. community with the ultimate fusion of print and web journalism. Founded in 1978 by an investment group that included actor Michael Douglas and journalist Jay Levin among others, *L.A. Weekly* is the nation's mostly widely read alt-weekly, with well over four million active users visiting laweekly.com each month. Nationally, the *Weekly* has won more awards from the Association of Alternative Newsmedia than any other publication in the country. Steve Friess is an American freelance journalist, blogger, and podcaster based in Las Vegas whose work appears regularly in the *Politico Pro, The New York Times, USA Today, Newsweek,* the *Los Angeles Times,* Wired.com, *The Daily Beast*, and others.

Statesman Journal was founded in 1851 in Salem, Oregon. Now owned by Gannett, the parent company of *USA Today*, the daily newspaper maintains a left political bias.

Tannehill, Brynn. "The Truth About Transgender Suicide." *Huffington Post*. November 14, 2015. *Huffington Post* is an American news and opinion website and blog, with localized and international editions. Founded in 2005 by Arianna Huffington, Kenneth Lerer, and Jonah Peretti it is edited from a left wing political perspective. The site offers news, satire, blogs, and original content and covers politics, business, entertainment, environment, technology, popular media, lifestyle, culture, comedy, healthy living, women's interests, and local news. Brynn Tannehill, originally from Phoenix, Arizona graduated from the Naval Academy in 1997 with a B.S. in computer science. She earned her Naval Aviator wings in 1999 and flew SH-60B helicopters and P-3C maritime patrol aircraft during three deployments between 2000 and 2004. She was a campaign analyst while deployed overseas to 5th Fleet Headquarters in Bahrain from 2005 to 2006. In 2008, Brynn earned an M.S. in Operations Research from the Air Force Institute of Technology and transferred from active duty to the Naval Reserves. In 2008, Brynn began working as a senior defense research scientist in private industry. She left the drilling reserves and began transition in 2010. Since then she has written for *OutServe* magazine, *The New Civil Rights Movement*, and *Queer Mental Health* as a blogger and featured columnist. Brynn and her wife Janis currently live in Xenia, Ohio, with their three children.

Wadler, Joyce, "The Lady Regrets." *New York Times*, February 2, 2007. *The New York Times* is an American newspaper founded in 1851. Based in New York City, *The Times* is ranked eighteenth in the world by circulation and third in the US. Its editorial stance is left wing. Joyce Wadler is a journalist and reporter for *The New York Times* as well as a writer and humorist.

RADIO PROGRAMS

Richard Harris, "Search for 'Gay Genes' Comes up Short in Large New Study." National Public Radio "All Things Considered," August 29, 2019, National Public Radio. NPR is a non-profit organization with both public and private funding. It is based in Washington, D.C., and maintains a left of center bias. An award-winning journalist and science desk correspondent, Richard Harris has reported on a wide range of topics in science, medicine, and the environment since he joined NPR in 1986. In early 2014, his focus shifted from an emphasis on climate change and the environment to biomedical research.